Modern Critica

J. R. R. TOLKIEN

Edited and with an introduction by
Harold Bloom
Sterling Professor of the Humanities
Yale University

CHELSEA HOUSE PUBLISHERS
Philadelphia

10 9 8 7 6 5 4 3 2

∞ The paper used in this publication meets the minimum
requirements of the American National Standard for
Permanence of Paper for Printed Library Materials,
Z39.48-1984

Library of Congress Cataloging-in-Publication Data

J. R. R. Tolkien / edited and with an introduction
by Harold Bloom.
        p. cm.— (Modern critical views)
     Includes bibliographical references and index.
     ISBN 0-7910-5660-0 (alk. paper)
     1. Tolkien, J. R. R. (John Ronald Reuel), 1892–1973—
Criticism and interpretation.   2. Fantasy fiction,
English—History and criticism.   3. Middle Earth
(Imaginary place) I. Title: J. R. R. Tolkien. II. Bloom,
Harold. III. Series.
PR6039.O32 Z56   2000
828'.91209—dc21   99-051326
                                              CIP

Contributing Editor: Aaron Tillman

Contents

Editor's Note

My Introduction is a brief appreciation of *The Hobbit*, and of the personality of the amiable Bilbo Baggins.

Thomas J. Gasque takes exception to such Tolkienesque blunders as Tom Bombadil (who is a bore) and the two egregious monsters, the Balrog and Shelab.

Paul H. Kocher is heartened by Tolkien's epic "paean to hope," after which Roger Sale makes an epic defense of Tolkien's "heroic" achievement.

Biography of Tolkien is provided by Daniel Grotta-Kurska, while Timothy R. O'Neill compounds poor Tolkien with Carl Gustaf Jung.

Anne C. Petty subsumes *The Hobbit* into patterns of the folk-tale, after which Paul H. Kocher returns to expound the rather dense mythology of *The Silmarillion*.

Neil D. Isaacs argues the need for more informed criticism of Tolkien, while T. A. Shippey usefully provides some philological information.

Science fiction is invoked as a useful context for Tolkien in the essay by Richard L. Purtill that concludes this volume.

Introduction

J. R. R. Tolkien was a distinguished scholar of Anglo-Saxon literature, particularly of the epic poem *Beowulf*. His greater fame resulted from his fantasy-romance *The Lord of the Rings*, which I have reread with care and with considerable aesthetic reservations. Since I also have just reread *The Hobbit*, prelude to the larger work, with pleasure, and am more persuaded by it than by *The Lord of the Rings*, I will devote this Introduction only to *The Hobbit* (1937). My views on *The Lord of the Rings* (1954–55), such as they are, constitute my Introduction to the volume on *The Lord of the Rings* in the Chelsea House series MODERN CRITICAL INTERPRETATIONS, published simultaneously with *J. R. R. Tolkien* in MODERN CRITICAL VIEWS.

The Hobbit continues to be a story written for extremely intelligent children of all ages, and Bilbo Baggins seems to me easier to accept and like than is his heroic nephew, Frodo Baggins, the protagonist of the long and complicated *The Lord of the Rings*. Bilbo Baggins, though an admirable hobbit, is fortunately more a well-meaning burglar than he is a hero. I think we are fond of him because he is a hobbit to whom things happen. But Frodo Baggins makes things happen, and is certainly heroic, and I, at least, don't always understand how I am to judge his heroism, even when I am instructed by Roger Sale, certainly the best of all Tolkien critics. But that is an argument for the Introduction to the companion volume of this book.

Bilbo Baggins's preferences for comfort and a sleepy existence persuade because of their universality. Warring against goblins may be an exemplary occupation for others, but not for one's self, and it always seems better when goblins are kept away from the world of what Freud called Reality-Testing or the necessity for (eventually) dying. *The Hobbit* remains a rather funny book, so long as it gives primacy to Bilbo's good sense that adventures are "wretched, tiresome, uncomfortable." Dragons, I feel, ought to have no place in Bilbo's life; he is too amiable to be bothered by them. That is probably Tolkien's best joke in *The Hobbit*; we keep being rueful at all

1

the perils Bilbo is dragged into, though without them there would be no tale to tell. If trolls and goblins are going about, we want Bilbo to be safe in his wonderfully comfortable hobbit-hole, and I am rather grateful to Tolkien that sometimes I want to be there with Bilbo, even though I know only a few trolls and no goblins whatsoever.

I suspect that *The Lord of the Rings* is fated to become only an intricate Period Piece, while *The Hobbit* may well survive as Children's Literature. Really good-natured fantasy is hard to come by, and one convincing personality at its center is all it requires. No other figure in *The Hobbit* can be called a personality, but Bilbo Baggins is so vivid and persistent that he makes up for all the others. The first thing we hear Bilbo say is "Good morning!" to the self-important wizard, Gandalf, who is rude enough to over-interpret the remark. Bilbo's last exclamation is also to Gandalf, who has become more respectful and even fond of Mr. Baggins by the end of the book, but still feels compelled to remind him that "you are only quite a little fellow in a wide world after all!" Charming as always, Bilbo comforts us with a laughing "Thank goodness!"

THOMAS J. GASQUE

Tolkien: The Monsters and the Critters

In his 1936 Gollancz Memorial Lecture, J. R. R. Tolkien makes this curious and not fully elaborated statement:

> It is the strength of the northern mythological imagination that
> . . . put the monsters in the centre, gave them victory but no
> honour, and found a potent but terrible solution in naked will
> and courage. . . . So potent is it, that while the older southern
> imagination has faded for ever into literary ornament, the
> northern has power, as it were, to revive its spirit even in our
> own times.

What Tolkien may well have had in his mind when he spoke of the "power . . . to revive its spirit . . . in our own times" was his own use of the northern imagination in *The Hobbit*, which he had already written, and in *The Lord of the Rings*, which was probably well under way at that time. Perhaps Tolkien was justifying his revival of the spirit in the same way that much of his essay "On Fairy-Stories" seems to be slanted toward a defense of his own work as well as of the genre. The defense is convincing, however, and one critic has used the essay to show how Tolkien has created, by his own definition, a successful fairy story.

From *Tolkien and the Critics: Essays on J. R. R. Tolkien's The Lord of the Rings*, edited by Neil D. Isaacs and Rose A. Zimbardo. © 1968 by University of Notre Dame Press.

Although at times the landscape literally comes to life, in a geographical sense Middle-earth is hardly fantastic. Rather what really makes Tolkien's province a world of its own is the large population of sundry creatures, for Tolkien has put the monster—and the critters—at the center of his story, and it is they who provide the interest.

As a philologist and medieval scholar, Tolkien is steeped in traditional northern mythology; he has drawn on this lore in creating his characters and in refashioning a genre: ". . . he [Tolkien] has so profoundly penetrated the spirit of a genre that he has created a modern work in its mode" ⟨Edmund Fuller, *The Lord of the Hobbits: J. R. R. Tolkien*⟩. Although Roger Sale disagrees, I feel that, excepting the hobbits, Tolkien's fanciful elements are most successful when they are rooted in the traditional. In *The Hobbit* Tolkien's dragon was a dragon was a dragon, and the dragon as monster succeeds there in a way that whole shoals of Balrogs and Shelobs never would. It is not the fantastic monsters, fearful though they may be, but the dwarfs, elves, and even the orcs that give the greatest vitality to the work. And it is largely because of the traditional associations that they so succeed.

But the tradition can also be a hindrance, especially when it is inconsistent, as in the case of elves. Sometime around the sixteenth century the idea of an elf changed from a man-sized creature to one who could hide in a cowslip. The diminutive nature of elves, Tolkien suggests, is "largely a sophisticated product of literary fancy." The word "*elf*," he notes in the appendix, "has been diminished, and to many it may now suggest fancies either pretty or silly. . . ." Elves "were tall, fair of skin and grey-eyed, though their looks were dark, save in the golden house of Finrod." This garbled tradition perhaps makes it difficult for the reader—at least it did for me—to visualize these creatures, and even after the appearance of Glorfindel, I had trouble disposing of the idea of tiny elves. The goblins of *The Hobbit* also evidence this hindrance. That Tolkien changed their names to orcs in the trilogy suggests that he saw in the word "goblin" overtones of harmless children on Halloween and chose a less familiar and hence less diminished name.

The tradition of a race of creatures beyond the human pale, then, is inconsistent. Although in traditional elf or dwarf lore there is general agreement, the stock is far from pure. When we attempt to arrange the folk of Faërie into a systematic structure, says Thomas Keightley, "we find the foundation crumbling under our feet." In order to build a structure, Tolkien has selected those materials that make the system consistent. This is, of course, an artist's prerogative. Tolkien is not offering us *the* system of Faërie; he is offering us his own system—a new building made from the old lumber. But we must become aware of this structure gradually if we are to perceive its inner consistency and to accept what we see. Thus Tolkien must provide a bridge from the world of trees, birds, and ordinary people to the world of elves and dragons. In his fairy-story essay, he commented that the dream-frame is a trick, as bad as a time-machine, and one does better if he plunges his reader right into the middle of his imaginary world. In the trilogy, he does this for the hobbits by making no apologies for having created them. But because hobbits are just a little different from ordinary people and because these differences only slowly make themselves felt, we tend to accept totally the variants in their character delineation.

Hobbits, excepting Bilbo, are just as provincial in the Shire as people are on the earth and have little awareness of what the land beyond the Brandywine contains. The broad scope of Middle-earth unfolds slowly and believably for us as we cross the bridge from a known world to a fabulous one. Early in the work, we hear the Shirefolk discuss the land beyond the Brandywine, which in retrospect seems to us so tame, as a mysterious place, "where folks are so queer."

> 'And no wonder they're queer,' put in Daddy Twofoot . . . , 'if they live on the wrong side of the Brandywine River, and right agin the Old Forest. That's a dark bad place, if half the tales be true.'

Somewhat later, after we have accepted the existence not only of hobbits but even of Gandalf the Wizard and of dwarfs, Tolkien drops us in on another tavern conversation, at *The Green Dragon*:

> 'Queer things you do hear these days, to be sure,' said Sam.
> 'Ah,' said Ted, 'you do, if you listen. But I can hear fireside-tales and children's stories at home, if I want to.'
> 'No doubt you can,' retorted Sam, 'and I daresay there's more truth in some of them than you reckon. Who invented the stories anyway? Take dragons now.'
> 'No thank 'ee,' said Ted, 'I won't. I heard tell of them when I was a youngster, but there's no call to believe in them now. There's only one Dragon in Bywater, and that's Green,' he said, getting a general laugh.

Then Sam brings up the matter of elves and recalls old tales of elf-ships sailing west from the Grey Havens, leaving the folk of Middle-earth. "'Let them sail!'" says Ted. "'But I warrant you haven't seen them doing it.'" Sam had not, but he "believed he had once seen an Elf in the woods, and still hoped to see more one day."

Such is the mental state of the average hobbit-on-the-street, who is almost, but not quite, ready to believe in fabulous creatures. This previous scene and the credibility of the hobbits are a preparation for the first meeting with elves in the Green-Hill Country in the southern part of the Shire.

If elves are fantastic and unreal creatures, dwarfs are not; they are merely "outlandish folk . . . with long beards and deep hoods," who create a mild surprise at Bywater when they drive in with a load of birthday presents. Tolkien has asked us, then, to accept hobbits and dwarfs without question, and with the help of Sam's qualified credulity, we as readily accept the elves. The Black Riders are ambiguous enough at first, so that we have believed in them as real men before they are confirmed as Wraiths.

Not until we meet Tom Bombadil in the Old Forest do we face our first problem of belief. The lack of preparation for such a scene and its being followed by the episode at Bree, back in the normal world, mark Tolkien's technical failure, and hence it is a charming but slightly unconvincing digression, much less effective than the organic and fascinating episode in Fangorn with the Ents. The failure of the Bombadil episode happens, thinks Roger Sale, because it is an "invention" rather than a "creation" and never really comes alive. "As a result the unfriendly reader finds an easy stopping place in Tom Bombadil; forty pages of such dull stuff so early in a long work is hard to get over."

In addition to Tom Bombadil, there are in the trilogy two other important creatures—both of them monsters—who are different in conception and, we might say, in psychology from any of the others. They are the Balrog and Shelob. Most of the other creatures are more or less "human," with human-like motives and responses. The use of superficially nonhuman beings is Tolkien's method of characterization: "Much that in a realistic work would be done by 'character delineation' is here done simply by making the character an elf, a dwarf, or a hobbit. The imagined beings have their insides on the outside; they are visible souls." But this is not true of Tom, of the Balrog, or of Shelob; they are entirely nonhuman and seem to represent natural rather than psychological forces. Bombadil is apparently some kind of nature god, or perhaps he is the embodiment of the life principle. His incantations alone can dispel the force of the Barrow-wight, who perhaps represents death; these incantations apparently revitalize nature and thus overcome death. The dark, grave-like abode of the Wight is in sharp contrast to the "clean grass" outside where Tom takes Frodo. Regardless of what we think the meaning of Tom Bombadil is, he probably is not intended as a "character delineation," for he is even less human than the Ents.

Tom shares at least one characteristic with the two monsters: his indifference to the ring. For him, as for the Balrog and Shelob, it has no power to do either good or evil. He is interested only in sustaining life and fostering the enjoyment of it; they care only for destruction or, in Shelob's case, for satisfying the appetite. And none of the three willingly acknowledges any other creature as his master. All three possess an independence that places them outside the central moral concern of the story—the destruction of the Ring. Their amorality, like their nonhumanity, reveals them as allegorical principles: Tom of life or nature, Shelob of death or blind appetite, and the Balrog of a central disorder that no creature can withstand.

We could object to Tolkien's inclusion of Bombadil and the two monsters because they are principles rather than personalities. But allegory in a work of this sort need not be an artistic failure. Tolkien does fail with these two, however, not because he chose to dehumanize them, but because he failed to make them convincing. Treebeard, for example, is much more interesting than Tom Bombadil, and the orcs more fearsome than the Balrog.

Although we could not call the adventures with the Balrog and with Shelob dull, they both seem to fail, not in execution but in conception. Tolkien has invented these monsters rather than created them from the raw material of folklore as he did his other creatures. We are unable to believe in the Balrog because we have no foundation either outside the work or in it. Dwarfs, orcs, and elves are familiar enough to most readers to stimulate a response. Other creatures, including hobbits, the Ringwraiths, and the Dark Lord himself are fully developed within the trilogy. Not so with the Balrog. There he is, all of a sudden, whiffling and burbling, a *Diabolus ex machina*, when the orcs were foe enough. He is not dull, but the excitement is on the surface, and we only half believe Gandalf when he cries, "'Fly! This is a foe beyond any of you.'"

Shelob is better executed than her counterpart, but both episodes are artistically weak. For sheer terror, they are on a level with the invention of dozens of science-fiction writers, but terror is not enough. Nor is the argument that only such supernatural creatures could cause Gandalf's death or Frodo's paralysis, for there is still the feeling that these demons are not real. They are unreal because they are extraneous to the traditional framework of the story.

I think that Tolkien failed with his extra-fabulous monsters because he himself did not believe in them. On the other hand, he did, and still does, believe in elves, dwarfs, hobbits, orcs, and Ents, and it is these, along with the men, who really come alive. And a good portion of this vitality comes, I think, not just from the author's potent imagination, but from a combination of that with the centuries-old traditions in the northern mind which are capable of endless revitalization.

That Tolkien believes in elves, or in the idea of Faërie, the realm of fairies, is inferred from his fairy-story essay. And that he believes that there is a spirit which dwells in growing things is suggested by his Introductory

Note to *Tree and Leaf*. A neighbor's poplar tree was cut down for the crime of being "large and alive. I do not think it had any friends, or any mourners, except myself and a pair of owls." I do not of course mean that Tolkien is so naive as to believe in them in the same way that he would believe in, say, elephants or termites. Rather, it is a state of mind, a quality of kinship with a primal essence and with nature. Thus it is that his characters who are on the side of good are closely identified with and appreciate nature, and those on the bad are associated with barrenness and are hostile to growing things. This contrast is first developed in Tom Bombadil and the Barrow-wight. Sam the gardener is opposed to Ted Sandyman the miller, whose new mill in the Sharkey regime looms up "in all its frowning and dirty ugliness: a great brick building straddling the stream, which it fouled with a steaming and stinking outflow." Among the wizards, Gandalf is friend to the forests and to Bombadil, but Saruman, according to Treebeard, "has a mind of metal and wheels; and he does not care for growing things, except as far as they serve him for the moment." This rather oversimplified relationship between good and evil seems to be without exception.

Since hobbits and Ents are essentially Tolkien's creations, not inventions, I shall look more closely at elves, dwarfs, and orcs. Though no broadly inclusive category can be drawn for dwarfs and elves, some generalizations can be made. In Norse folklore, where these creatures are most fully developed, elves were generally thought of as good and friendly to men. Dwarfs, on the other hand, were less esteemed, for they frequently sought to do mischief to men. Trolls were a larger manifestation of the dwarf family. Elves, as in Tolkien, prefer forest-homes, while dwarfs live in hills or in the ground and sometimes under water. They are traditionally masters of metallurgy, and many of the swords of mythology were forged by them. There seems to be little tradition for elves as craftsmen, although Tolkien's elves fashioned the Rings of power and Aragorn's sword.

Tolkien's dwarfs are, in the main, traditional. In addition to their diminutive size, their underground homes, and their craftsmanship, they have a monarchical social order, have great stores of wealth, and are gifted with great strength. Tolkien makes use of all of these characteristics. There is an interesting divergence, however. Dwarfs in folklore are more often than not mounted on steeds, suited to their size, but Gimli is afraid of horses and would rather walk. Perhaps he is simply wary of such a large one as that offered by the Rohirrim, for he clings to Legolas as nervously as "Sam Gamgee in a boat."

The enmity between elves and dwarfs does not seem to be traditional, but Tolkien has created a long-standing feud between the two races and has made effective use of it. Legolas the elf is a creature of the woods and Gimli of the ground. The friendship which they eventually develop is a significant fusion of two elements of nature, already largely fused in the hobbits, who live in the ground and cultivate plants. The friendship of the elf and the dwarf is sealed when they convince each other of the beauty of the realms they each love. They make a bargain that Legolas will visit the caverns and Gimli the Forest of Fangorn, each to enjoy the unaccustomed beauties.

Of the significant creatures, the orcs remain. What they are is never really clear. Treebeard says they were made by "the Enemy in the Great Darkness, in mockery of . . . Elves," just as trolls are counterfeits of Ents. There is ample tradition to support the existence of such beasts; certain variants in dwarf lore were known as Cornish mine goblins—"'miserable, little, withered, dried up creatures'" with "'big, ugly heads with red or grey locks, squintan [sic] eyes, hook noses, and mouths from ear to ear.'" Another, more flexible, tradition is the generally later medieval concept of the Wild Man, which abounds in medieval art. He was "a hairy man curiously compounded of human and animal traits, without, however, sinking to the level of an ape." He is that same wild man whose character was ameliorated into the Noble Savage, but in the Middle Ages, he was merely a savage, incapable of intelligent speech, of upright posture, and of Grace.

Medieval theologians had considerable difficulty in accounting for the wild man, since he did not seem to belong on the Chain of Being as a separate species. Therefore, they viewed his state as psychological rather than theological, brought to his condition by loss of mind or extreme hardship. He was thus not totally beyond Grace. It is clear that Gollum, perhaps Tolkien's most delightfully disgusting creation, fits this pattern. The wild man, like Gollum, usually lived alone, had no use for metallurgy, and ate berries, acorns, and raw flesh. Gollum also is in a depraved condition as a result of having lost his humanity, and his salvation, or rather the Middle-earth equivalent of it, is not entirely impossible.

But wild men were not all bad. Unlike the creatures of evil in the trilogy, they had a close identification with nature, and a wild man's life was often bound up with the life of a certain tree. Furthermore, they were good with animals and were often thought of as herdsmen. In some cases, especially when the state of wildness was intermittent—love sickness a cause more often than not—the wild man was a dispenser of wisdom, for he gleaned secrets from the forces of nature. Merlin, in some of the legends, was such a one.

It is partially in the framework of this broad and flexible tradition that Tolkien created orcs. Even the name of that evil race is in tradition. It is from the Italic god of death and the underworld, Orcus, from whom the French got the word *ogre*; and the word *orcus* occurs at least once in the Middle Ages referring specifically to the wild man. But again Tolkien uses the elements he wants to use and makes a creature of his own. The normally hermit-like wild man becomes the gregarious orc, but each orc is savagely selfish and shows little spirit of cooperation, he is the dark counterpart to the elf and the dwarf, cutting down trees and desecrating caves, a symbolic embodiment of those people the author calls "orc-minded," whose speech is "dreary and repetitive with hatred and contempt, too long removed from good to retain even verbal vigour, save in the ears of those to whom only the squalid sounds strong."

Tolkien, then, makes effective use of two kinds of tradition: first, that which is the common heritage of the whole culture, such as the elves and dwarfs, and his main adaptation of this is in his ordering of the tradition, his creation of a credible and organic system on which to structure his story. Second, he has adapted certain flexible traditions, like the wild man, to his own thematic pattern of good and evil, and to this extent he creates a tradition. Where his creations fail, they are outside the organic traditional pattern of Tolkien's world, not simply because they do not belong there but because they seem to be in another plane of existence, as out of place as a time machine. But when he succeeds, he does so beautifully, and his creatures are as real as a next-door neighbor. Hobbits, for all I know, may be still around, just "hard to find," dwarfs may be still in the hills, and the elves may only be waiting for another age, there where they sailed from the Grey Havens to the land beyond the sea.

PAUL H. KOCHER

Cosmic Order

Tolkien is not a philosopher or a theologian but a literary artist who thinks. Consequently he is not content merely to narrate a bare series of events but surrounds each high point of the action in *The Lord of the Rings* with convictions and opinions expressed by the participants as to its possible place in some larger plan under execution by greater hands than theirs. Their speculations on such a topic could easily lead to the familiar vexing, futile debates on predestination, foreknowledge, contingent futures, free will, and the rest of that thorny thicket. Tolkien, however, refuses to weigh down his story by letting his people think or talk like professionals in these areas. Virtually without exception the elves, men, hobbits, and their allies of the West come to believe in a moral dynamism in the universe to which each of them freely contributes, without exactly knowing how, and without being at all sure how it will eventually work out in the war against Sauron. But they eschew technical terms and discuss each crisis not as an intellectual problem but as a stern occasion demanding concrete choices and chances. Being thoughtful people, though, they say quite enough in the process to give a good idea of the kind of order in which they believe and the nature of the planner operating through it.

The first serious discussion about these matters takes place early in Part I, Book I, when Gandalf explains to Frodo what the Ring is and how Bilbo

From *Master of Middle-earth: The Fiction of J. R. R. Tolkien* by Paul H. Kocher. © 1972 by Paul H. Kocher.

came to get it from Gollum in the caverns under the Misty Mountains: "Bilbo's arrival just at that time, and putting his hand on it, blindly, in the dark" was not the accident it seems but "the strangest event in the whole history of the Ring so far." At the call of Sauron's will his Ring was leaving Gollum to return to its maker, but Bilbo found it because "there was something else at work beyond any design of the Ring-maker. I can put it no plainer than by saying that Bilbo was *meant* to find the Ring, and *not* by its maker. In which case you also were *meant* to have it." Plainly Gandalf is saying that the "something else" which thwarted Sauron was stronger than he and used this recall of the Ring as a means of putting it, instead, into the possession of the Dark Lord's enemies through Bilbo. This intervention, coming just at this juncture, is crucial. Control of the Ring gives the West its one slim chance of defeating Sauron. Had the Ring remained with Gollum, or even stayed lost, Sauron's armies were strong enough to win easily without it, as everyone admits. The free peoples can overcome him only by destroying the Ring, and with it the vigor which he himself poured into it in the Second Age, and which is still necessary to his hold on life in Middle-earth. Bilbo's picking up the Ring in the dark is the first step on the long road to Mount Doom.

No conscious choice of Bilbo's led to his finding the Ring. He did not even know what it was at the time. But the incident did require of him a decision whether or not to kill Gollum. Out of pity he freely chose not to kill, a choice highly commended by Gandalf, which won Bilbo the personal "reward" of taking little hurt from the evil of the Ring. More importantly, Gandalf guesses, he knows not how, that Gollum is "bound up with the fate of the Ring," and that he "has some part to play yet, for good or ill, before the end." This can only be a piece of inspired foresight on Gandalf's part, however vague its content. He has no rational way of knowing that only Gollum, stumbling down into the Cracks of Doom with the Ring, will save it from Sauron at the last moment and accomplish his destruction.

Many of the wise on Middle-earth have such general glimpses of the future, but they are never more than vague and unspecific. The future is the property of the One who plans it. Yet is it fixed in the sense that every link in the chain of its events is foreordained? It cannot be, because in his encounter with Gollum Bilbo's choice to kill or not to kill is genuinely free, and only after it has been made is it woven into the guiding scheme. Tolkien leaves it at that. Human (or hobbitic or elvish or dwarfish or entish) free will coexists with a providential order and promotes this order, not frustrates it.

Gandalf has said that Bilbo was "meant" to find the Ring in order to pass it on to Frodo as his heir. Frodo was "meant" to bear it from then on. But Gandalf does not assume that Frodo will necessarily do what he was intended to, though he should. When Frodo, rebelling at first against the duty imposed on him, asks the natural question, "Why was I chosen?" the wizard can only reply that nobody knows why; Frodo can be sure only that it was not because of any surpassing merits he has: "But you have been chosen, and you must therefore use such strength and heart and wits as you have." The reasons why one instrument is "chosen" rather than another are not outwardly visible to any eyes on Middle-earth. Yet Gandalf carefully goes on to inform Frodo that he is free to accept or reject the choice: ". . . the decision lies with you." The option not to cooperate with the grand design is open to Frodo's will, as it is to that of all other intelligent creatures who are aware of the issues. Frodo groans but takes up his appointed burden. Sam later does the same on the trip to Rivendell when he tells Frodo: ". . . I have something to do before the end, and it lies ahead, not in the Shire. I must see it through . . ." It is no business of Tolkien's to tell us what would have happened had these choices been refused by the hobbits. We are left at liberty to presume that other persons would have taken their place. For it is becoming clear that the designer is working against Sauron and would, if necessary, have brought forward alternative means to confound him.

This impression is strongly fortified by a passage in Appendix B defining the mission of the five wizards, led by Gandalf and Saruman, to Middle-earth, as understood by later chroniclers: "It was afterwards said that they came out of the Far West and were messengers sent to contest the power of Sauron, and to unite all those who had the will to resist him; but they were forbidden to match his power with power, or to seek to dominate Elves or Men by force and fear . . . They came therefore in the shape of men . . ." Who "sent" them and who "forbad"? Surely it was either the Valar or the One who established them as guardians of Middle-earth and whose design they were charged to administer. It says a good deal about the character of that designer that he cared enough about the future of Middle-earthly peoples to send messengers to help them against evil and yet confined that help to education and persuasion, leaving their wills unforced. Stress is put on the moral side of the struggle against Sauron and on each person's right to select his own role, or lack of any role, in it. Being either one of the Valar himself or at least instructed by them, Gandalf knows as much as any creature can when he suggests a personal will that "means" and "chooses" as it works out its design. And no less so when he reminds all comers that they are the final masters of their own decisions, though what the consequences will be is not for them to know.

Gandalf had intended to escort the Ring-bearer to Rivendell to guard him from Sauron's agents along the way. Tolkien first strips Frodo of protection through Saruman's imprisonment of Gandalf and then restores it by Frodo's apparently accidental encounter with Gildor's elves just as he is about to be attacked by Black Riders. Gildor, knowing how rare the meetings of elves with other creatures in the woods are, suspects a hidden intention behind this one: "In this meeting there may be more than chance; but the purpose is not clear to me, and I fear to say too much." Being no more informed than anyone else on Middle-earth of the aims of this "purpose," the elf is reluctant to give any advice that may unduly influence Frodo's choices and so make them less free. What he can and does do is pass along to "those that have power to do good" the news that the hobbits are in peril. So warned, Bombadil, and later Aragorn, arrive at critical moments as substitutes for Gandalf to give them the aid which he cannot give.

Frodo himself raises the question whether his rescue by Bombadil from Old Man Willow was only happenstance: "Did you hear me calling, Master, or was it just chance that brought you at that moment?" Tom's answer is both yea and nay, but the yea is louder. He did not hear Frodo calling for help, and he was on an errand that afternoon which took him to that part of the Old Forest to gather waterlilies. On the other hand, he had been alerted by Gildor that the hobbits were in need and he was watching the danger spots. In sum, says Tom, "Just chance brought me then, if chance you call it. It was no plan of mine, though I was waiting for you." The incredulous "if chance you call it" tends to deny that the rescue was really chance, however mortals may commonly define the concept. "It was no plan of mine" invites the thought that there was a plan, though it was not his. Questions of this sort are meant to live on in the back of the reader's mind and to make him doubt that Aragorn's very opportune appearance later on at a time of maximum danger in the inn at Bree is as fortuitous as it seems.

Tolkien is here facing a joint literary-philosophical imperative. Literarily, he wants to keep an atmosphere of wonder at the mysterious hand which is guiding events, but he must not let this theme become so strong or definite as to persuade his readers that the hobbits are certain to reach Rivendell safely. To do so would be fatal to the suspense, and therefore to the story as story. Philosophically, if the guiding hand is really to guide effectively, it must have power to control events, yet not so much as to take away from the people acting them out the capacity for moral choice. The latter, being fundamental to Tolkien's conception of man (and other rational beings), must be preserved at all costs. So Tolkien cannot allow his cosmic order to be a fixed, mechanistic, unchangeable chain of causes and effects. The order must be built flexibly around creaturely free will and possible personal providential interventions from on high.

Tolkien uses several techniques to attain the desired balances. For one thing he never speaks about these matters as author, and thereby avoids authorial certitudes. His characters may be certain, or virtually so, that a providential order is at work but they are never sure of its final outcome, or exactly how it operates. Witness Gandalf, who is positive that the Ring was "meant" to fall into the hands of the West but not what its future is to be after that, and who guesses that Gollum has a part yet to play but knows not whether it is for good or ill. Witness also Gildor, who intuits a supervening purpose in his meeting with the hobbits but confesses his ignorance of its aims. And Bombadil, who, while intimating that his rescue of Frodo was not coincidence, regards himself as ultimately outside the contending forces in the War of the Ring.

Another technique Tolkien finds handy is to couple every incident anyone calls foreordained with some notable exercise of free will by one of the characters involved in it. For example, as noted, Bilbo and Frodo are said to be chosen as Ring-bearers, but Bilbo is given the option to spare or kill Gollum, and Frodo can always decline to serve. This duality is repeated again and again straight through to the end of the epic. Yet another device is to let most of the major characters voice premonitions or prophecies, seeming to entail a definite foreseeable future, yet to keep these either misty in content or tentative in tone, so loosening their fixity and hinting that the routes are various by which they may come true.

All these devices Tolkien handles with persuasive tact. But they are successful also because they create for life on Middle-earth a kind of atmosphere that our own existential experience of living accepts as genuine. Very common for us is the sense that our lives are bound in with larger patterns that we cannot change. Yet tomorrow seems never sure, and at every new crossroads nothing is stronger than the feeling inside us that we are the masters of our alternatives.

Because Elrond's Council is a turning point in the history of Middle-earth and because he himself, with Gandalf and Galadriel, is the wisest of the assembled leaders of the West, his solemn opening statement to them that some force greater than themselves has brought them together at this crisis carries special weight. To decide what to do with the Ring, he says, "That is the purpose for which you are called hither. Called, I say, though I have not called you to me, strangers from distant lands. You have come and are here met, in this very nick of time, by chance as it may seem. Yet it is not so. Believe rather that it is so ordered that we who sit here, and none others, must now find counsel for the perils of the world." Nothing could be plainer than Elrond's rejection here of chance as the cause of the Council, however much on the surface it may seem to be so. Almost as plain is his language pointing to the personal nature of the summoner. Words like *purpose, called* (thrice spoken), *ordered, believe* look to some living will and even have a distantly Christian aura. Moreover, whoever did the calling was concerned for the West's welfare in the struggle against Sauron. Yet the whole purpose of assembling its leaders was not to force any course of action upon them but to have them freely debate it for themselves. The conclusions of the Council are not predetermined in any way, though its summoning was. Noteworthy also is the care with which Elrond avoids giving the supreme being any of the traditional names for God.

The Council having agreed at length that the Ring must be carried back to Mordor to be destroyed, a silence ensues until Frodo, overcoming "a great dread," speaks up with an effort to offer himself as carrier. This is the vocabulary of free choice. Elrond accepts it as such while at the same time believing that the same power that convoked the Council has also appointed Frodo to undertake the task. He sees no clash between the two ideas: "If I understand aright all that I have heard . . . I think that this task is appointed for you, Frodo; and that if you do not find a way, no one will . . . But it is a heavy burden . . . I do not lay it on you. But if you take it freely, I will say that your choice is right . . ." Though Frodo is a chosen instrument most likely to succeed, it is not a foregone conclusion that he will succeed. Providence, for its own reasons which finite minds cannot understand, may perhaps intend Sauron to win this bout in the never-ceasing war between good and evil. Elrond leaves the end open. Frodo has the right to accept or refuse the office as he wills, and no other person should tell him what to do. Yet refusal may bring unspoken penalties, since all acts have their consequences. If Frodo's acceptance would be "right," would not refusal be, if not "wrong," at least an abdication of duty, diminishing him morally? Much is implicit here. Among the natural inferences also is that Frodo's appointment to carry the Ring is of like kind with the selection of Bilbo and Frodo to find and receive it earlier, and was made by the same allseeing mind, in which Gandalf and Elrond, both pupils of the Valar, firmly believe.

Elrond here has ventured only a very generalized and conditional forecast of possible coming events. Gandalf's death in combat with the Balrog in Moria, however, is one of those main forks in the plot of which Aragorn as well as Gandalf has rather clear knowledge in advance. Aragorn is so sure beforehand of personal disaster to Gandalf that he insists on trying the alternate route over the Redhorn Gate first, and when they are forced by storm toward the old dwarf kingdom utters the strongest possible alarm to him: "I will follow your lead now—if this last warning does not move you . . . And I say to you: if you pass the doors of Moria, beware!" Aragorn does not say precisely what he fears, but the severity of his agitation can be for nothing less than Gandalf's death, and he accurately fears for no one else in the

Company, since all the rest are saved by Gandalf's sacrifice of himself. Gandalf, too, knows what awaits him. Rebuking Gimli weeks later for saying that the wizard's "foresight failed him" in entering Moria, Aragorn implies that Gandalf foreknew and accepted the result: "The counsel of Gandalf was not founded on foreknowledge of safety, for himself or others . . . There are some things that it is better to begin than to refuse, even though the end may be dark." But the inference also is that Gandalf could have chosen not to accept death, as Frodo could have chosen not to accept the Ring. The foreseen event will occur only *if* a creaturely will freely consents first. In this way Tolkien keeps his providential plan personalized, nonmechanistic, and not rigidly determined yet quite potent enough, withholds advance details about the precise shape and manner of the event foreknown, and, not incidentally, enhances the suspense of his tale.

Arrived at Lórien without Gandalf, the Company seeks the advice of Queen Galadriel, "greatest of Elven women" in Tolkien's phrase, whose life span extends back to the start of the First Age and whose wisdom is unexcelled among her race. But she is unexpectedly chary of making any predictions for them, or for the success of the West in general. She knows what is to come only "in part," she insists, and her mirror reveals not what shall be but only what "may be." Indeed she warns Frodo and Sam that what they see in its waters "is dangerous as a guide to deeds." It mixes up past, present, and future so indistinguishably that the gazer cannot be sure which is which, and in striving to avert a danger he thinks he sees lying ahead he may take the very measures which are necessary to bring it about. All finite knowledge about the future is cursed by this Oedipean paradox. Necessarily so, because it is incomplete and therefore blind in its information about the means which must precede any given consequence. What then? Are all flashes of foreknowledge false? Galadriel does not say so. But it is noticeable that she prefers to rely mostly on rational inferences from what she already knows about the past and present: "I will not give you counsel, saying do this, or do that. For not in doing or contriving, nor in choosing between this course and another, can I avail; but only in knowing what was and is, and in part also what shall be . . . Your Quest stands upon the edge of a knife . . . Yet hope remains while the Company is true."

This insight, couched in the most general terms, amounts in essence only to a statement of belief that if the members of the Company remain faithful to their trust they still have a chance. As in all previous instances, even so mild a prediction is made to depend upon their free obedience to moral laws. Later, Galadriel explicitly refuses to forecast whether Sauron will be overthrown: "I do not foretell, for all foretelling is now vain: on the one hand lies darkness, and on the other only hope," but she is willing to assure

Gimli that if he survives he will be rich, yet over him gold will not have the dominion it has over other dwarves. A likely enough conclusion from Gimli's stated preference for a strand of Galadriel's hair over all the gold and gems on earth. She is perhaps partly foreseeing, partly only comforting the Company when she urges them not to worry over their indecision about selection of a destination: "Maybe the paths that you each shall tread are already laid before your feet, though you do not see them." Nothing Galadriel says to them during their stay in Lórien shakes in any way the established doctrine of the epic that their future course is indeed laid out for them, provided they themselves choose to tread it. Her function in the story is to warn them, and herself, to tend to the duty in hand and not rashly to presume that finite minds can outguess the supreme architect who plans the whole.

Events bear out Galadriel's distrust of all creaturely foreknowledge, including her own. She proves to be only partly right in believing that the success of the Quest rests on the continued loyalty of everyone in the Company. At Parth Galen the evil desire for the Ring long growing in Boromir explodes into a physical attack on Frodo that splits the Company into groups, as it needs to be split, since each group has its own indispensable job to do in the complex campaigns that follow. Frodo, followed by Sam, is shocked into starting off by himself on the stealthy, inconspicuous course of slipping into Mordor in which lies his only possible chance of eluding Sauron's roving eye. Capture of Pippin and Merry by the orcs transports them to Fangorn Forest, where they escape just in time to rouse the ents to overwhelm Saruman at Isengard and Helm's Deep. Pursuing the captives, Aragorn meets Éomer, to begin the awakening of Rohan, and meets in the forest the reincarnated Gandalf who completes the process by freeing Théoden from Wormtongue. In consequence, Saruman's threat to Rohan is wiped out, and the Rohirrim have just enough time to send the army that saves Minas Tirith from the first onset of Sauron's hosts. Even this would not have been enough had Aragorn not been released by Saruman's defeat to ride the Paths of the Dead and so bring the armies of southern Gondor to the aid of the city when the Rohirrim faltered. None of this would have happened had not Boromir succumbed for a time to the spell of the Ring. In retrospect that evil hour was necessary to defeat evil in the long run as nothing else could have.

The momentum built up by Tolkien earlier for the existence of an unseen design behind all the episodes of his story carries forward into this long sequence of hairbreadth successes stemming from Boromir's fall. Even if Tolkien never said a further word about it we would be inclined to see the finger of Providence in them. But through various spokesmen, especially

Gandalf, he keeps up a running commentary to that effect. Hearing from Aragorn in Fangorn what happened at Parth Galen, Gandalf reflects on the unseen significance of the decision, made by Elrond only at the last moment, to include Merry and Pippin in the Company, which allowed Boromir to redeem himself by dying to protect them and which brought the ents into action: "It was not in vain that the young hobbits came with us, if only for Boromir's sake. But that is not the only part they have to play. They were brought to Fangorn, and their coming was like the falling of small stones that starts an avalanche in the mountains." He is using the same language he used to describe Gollum's "part" in the fate of the Ring. All are filling roles written for them by the same great playwright. And Gandalf has to laugh at the irony of the rival orc bands of Saruman and Sauron which captured the two hobbits, thereby serving to promote a good they never meant: "So between them our enemies have contrived only to bring Merry and Pippin with marvelous speed, and in the nick of time, to Fangorn, where otherwise they would never have come at all!" His own reincarnation he interprets as one more move in the plan, for he too has a role: "Naked I was sent back—for a brief time, until my task is done. And naked I lay upon the mountaintop," until an eagle sent by Galadriel brings him to Lórien for healing and consultation. The greater strength that the new White possesses as against the former Grey is needed for his coming labors, and he would never have had it, had not the Balrog first killed him down in the pit.

The irony of evil bringing forth good continues all through the epic. The flight of Wormtongue to his master Saruman seems at the time of no particular importance. But later, when Gandalf is parleying with Saruman at Orthanc, Wormtongue angrily tries to kill him by throwing down at him the precious *palantír* which Saruman would never willingly have parted with and which Gandalf could not have got by force from the impregnable tower, "Strange are the turns of fortune! Often does hatred hurt itself!" Gandalf is moved to exclaim. This is the *palantír* into which Pippin surreptitiously looks that night, to be saved partly by Sauron's sadistic urge to torture him in Mordor from having his mind read then and there by the telepathic Eye and all the strategy of the West ruinously exposed. "You have been saved, and all your friends too, mainly by good fortune, as it is called," remarks Gandalf, who does not believe in luck under any name. "As it is called" is reminiscent of Bombadil's "if chance you call it." Théoden expresses the awe of a more ordinary mortal: "Strange powers have our enemies, and strange weaknesses! . . . But it has long been said: *oft evil will shall evil mar.*" He too sees how the very qualities of evil are being turned against themselves for other ends. The idea has achieved the wide circulation of a proverb.

The true importance of Wormtongue's murderous impulse in hurling the *palantír*, however, is seen only when Aragorn claims possession of it as Elendil's rightful heir and with it purposely reveals himself to Sauron in order to frighten him into attacking Minas Tirith before his preparations are complete. Aragorn hopes that Sauron will believe that he has assumed the powers of the Ring and that the West must be overrun immediately before he has learned to wield them. Sauron is duly deceived. In Aragorn's place he would have seized the Ring long ago. The ripples of Aragorn's open challenge spread far and wide through the remainder of the story. Sauron never thereafter even suspects that anyone else may have the Ring, least of all Frodo, whom he regards as a petty spy even after his presence in Mordor becomes known. He does launch his armies against the city prematurely. The darkness with which he enshrouds everything spreads despair, certainly, but it also conceals Frodo's movements into Mordor as well as the coming of the cavalry of Rohan. Hasty emergence of the army under Angmar from Cirith Ungol leaves the mountain pass badly and confusedly guarded. Aragorn is enabled to take the pirates of Umbar unprepared. And so the consequences roll on through multitudinous incidents too many to detail but all working to the disadvantage of a mistakenly preoccupied Sauron.

The direst need for every sort of providential aid and the most direct and unequivocal answers to it come during Frodo and Sam's long ordeal in the dark in Mordor. What finally routs Shelob is a prayer to Elbereth in the elfin tongue, which springs into Sam's mind though he does not know the language. A similar prayer uttered by Sam and Frodo breaks the "will of the Watchers . . . with a suddenness like the snapping of a cord" and lets them escape from the Tower of Cirith Ungol. Meantime, Sam, having to decide whether he should "put himself forward" by taking over the Ring and the mission from the master he thinks dead, realizes that, like Frodo before him, he has "been put forward" by a higher power, must make up his own mind whether to ratify the choice, and does so.

Then, during a rest from pursuit by orcs, while Frodo sleeps, Sam looks up to see far above the murk "a white star twinkle." Smitten by its beauty he understands that "in the end the Shadow was only a small and passing thing: there was light and high beauty for ever beyond its reach." This is far more than the sighting of the physical beaming of a star. It is a spiritual vision of beauty and permanence which Sauron and his passing vileness can never stain. It puts everything into right perspective for Sam and gives him peace: "Now, for a moment, his own fate, and even his master's, ceased to trouble him." The world is in abler hands than his. A less visionary kind of help is sent later on the very slopes of Mount Doom when Sam has to carry Frodo and finds the burden light, "whether because Frodo was so

worn by his long pains . . . or because some gift of final strength was given . . ."
Tolkien guards the secular alternative but his favor is pretty clearly for the
religious one. Finally, of course, as Frodo succumbs to the ring at the Cracks
of Doom, Gollum, playing out the role for which he has been preserved all
through the epic, bites off Frodo's Ring-finger, overbalances (by no
accident), and falls with the Ring into the flames below. The irony of evil is
consummated by its doing the good which good could not do.

Providence, therefore, not only permits evil to exist but weaves it
inextricably into its purposes for Middle-earth. In the short term it may even
allow evil to triumph, and these short terms are often anything but short.
Morgoth's tyranny defies the best efforts of elves and men throughout the
thousands of years of the First Age until the Valar come against him. Sauron
wins again and again in the Second Age until conquered by Númenor, and
even then turns defeat into victory by seducing his conquerors into revolt
against the Valar. His temporary overthrow in the drowning of Númenor is
one which no doubt he would be delighted to repeat in the Third Age, since
he then took down with him into the darkness the highest civilization yet
achieved by man. Small wonder that with these terrible precedents behind
them, the Western leaders in the Third Age almost despair of winning the
War of the Ring. By its nature the cosmic order is directed toward good, and
in the long run those who cooperate with it must overcome, but who knows
how long the run is? Gandalf's retort to Denethor asserting that he too is a
steward accepts the possibility that Sauron will overrun the West: ". . . all
worthy things are in peril as the world now stands, those are my care. And
for my part I shall not wholly fail of my task, though Gondor should perish,
if anything passes through this night that can still grow fair or bear fruit and
flower again in days to come." Morning will come again and good will
flourish no matter how complete the devastation wrought by evil seems. This
is Gandalf's equivalent of Sam's vision of the star riding high above Mordor.

Nevertheless, the cost of even a passing victory by Sauron is so dreadful
as to call forth the united labors of the free peoples. He will not win if every
player accepts the part assigned. Hence the attempts of Gandalf and the rest
to educate every player in the importance of his role, freely enacted. Hence
also another moral strand, not yet dwelt upon, running from end to end of
the epic—the need of everyone in the West to resist the evil inherent in his
own nature. Too many Gollums, Boromirs, Sarumans, Denethors, and so on
would in effect turn the West into a second Númenor, corrupted and ripe for
another flood. Though not the only one, the Ring of course is the chief
instrument of temptation by its appeal to the evil within, an appeal made
sometimes directly to the baser desires, sometimes more subtly through
perversion of the loftiest instincts in the noblest minds.

As Tolkien writes his tale, he makes it one of the main objects of the providential order to test each of the major characters by putting the Ring within easy grasp if he will but reach out to seize it, or keep it, for himself. With Bilbo, who has the Ring to start with, the struggle is to give it up voluntarily to Frodo at Gandalf's urging. He barely succeeds. Isildur has failed before him. Then Frodo offers it to Gandalf, who vehemently refuses, well knowing that the Ring would turn to perverted ends the pity that is his most characteristic virtue. Aragorn's opportunity comes in the inn at Bree. The Ring is lawfully his, if anybody's, by inheritance from Isildur, and the hobbits are at his mercy. But he turns away and never turns back in all the weeks and months he spends in Frodo's company. This is his proof that he is worthy to be king. Elrond's rejection of the Ring took place ages before in the days of the Last Alliance, when he vainly urged Isildur under the walls of Barad-dûr to cast it into the nearby fires. Perhaps hardest of all is Galadriel's refusal to accept it when offered by Frodo in Lórien, because with it she could preserve the existence of that enchanted land which otherwise must pass away. In one of the great scenes of the epic she dreams aloud of what might be, then shatters the dream herself: "I pass the test . . . I will diminish, and go into the West, and remain Galadriel." More than the others she is aware that they are all being put to the proof. So the testing goes on, with Boromir at Parth Galen, Faramir in Ithilien, Sam in Mordor. Frodo's trial, of course, is as long as the epic and he does not come out of it unscathed. Among Western captains only Théoden, Saruman, and Denethor are not directly exposed to the fascination of the Ring. For them other tests are set up. Théoden must overcome the hopeless lassitude of old age intensified by Wormtongue. *Palantíri* are the proximate occasions for the falls of the other two.

For most of the participants on both sides of the War of the Ring the rewards of virtue or vice are simply the normal consequences flowing from victory or defeat. The free peoples are united to live under the just rule of their rightful King. Sauron's human allies are sent back to their home territories under binding treaties. His orcs, those that survive the slaughter, pen themselves in their caves under the mountains. A general purging of evil goes on. Though Sauron cannot be killed, his spirit is driven off the face of Middle-earth, forever to languish impotently in outer darkness. It is not altogether clear whether the same fate befalls Saruman. Coming originally from Valinor, his spirit in the form of a gray mist yearns westward when his body dies, "but out of the West came a cold wind, and it bent away, and with a sigh dissolved into nothing." This sounds like final dissolution, or at least final exile. Consumed in the volcanic explosions of Mount Doom, the Nazgûl perish at last and their spirits presumably go to that abyss that Gandalf warned Angmar was prepared for him, an almost total loss of being in "the nothingness that waits you and your Master." Denethor's final fate as a man is left doubtful. He kills himself in despair, disregarding the warning of Gandalf that suicide is forbidden: "Authority is not given to you, Steward of Gondor, to order the hour of your death . . . And only the heathen kings, under the Domination of the Dark Power, did thus, slaying themselves in pride and despair, murdering their kin to ease their own death." The flavor of this prohibition is distinctly religious, condemning the practice as "heathen" and ascribing it to pride and despair, mortal offenses in the lexicon of Christianity and other religions. Nothing is added, however, about punishments in an afterlife for Denethor or any other among the free peoples. The epic tends to avoid eschatology.

The leaving of Middle-earth by the elves is a special case. It is not connected with anything they have done or not done in the War of the Ring, but rather with their disobedience to the command of the Guardian Valar not to pursue Morgoth to Middle-earth in the early years of the First Age. The exile then imposed upon them as a punishment has been expiated by long years of struggle and suffering, their banishment has therefore been revoked, and their deeply implanted longing for their former lands in the Uttermost West is calling them home. As a further spur they have been told, or they foresee, that if they stay on Middle-earth they are destined to undergo a deterioration, "to forget and to be forgotten." The Fourth Age is intended by the One who decides such things to be an Age of Men. So they are returning to live with the Valar as they were meant to do from the beginning. Galadriel is forgiven by the Valar for her former defiances and allowed to accompany her elves overseas "in reward" for what she has done to oppose Sauron, "but above all for her rejection of the Ring when it came within her power." For their services involving the Ring, Bilbo and Frodo are the first hobbits to receive the unheard-of privilege of healing their wounds with the elves in the peace of the Undying Lands. Arwen, who has elected to become human by marrying Aragorn, is given the power to surrender to Frodo her seat in one of the boats sailing westward.

In all the foregoing arrangements of Peoples, and punishment or reward of individuals, the Valar are the immediate prime movers. But they are acting as executives of the will of the One, and their power of independent decision is limited. The Appendices tell of two pivotal events that reveal the outlines of these limits. When "as a reward for their sufferings in the cause against Morgoth, the Valar . . . granted to the Edain a land to dwell in . . ."—the island of Númenor, at the end of the First Age—they could triple the life spans of these men, but they could not make them undying as were the elves, because they *"were not permitted* to take from them the Gift of Men . . .": death (emphasis added). The Valar obeyed an edict coming down from above. On the other hand, they seem to have some discretion in applying this edict to the half-human, half-elven offspring of the two previous marriages between elves and men: "At the end of the First Age the Valar gave to the Half-elven an irrevocable choice to which kindred they would belong." Under the command to make this choice, Arwen abandons immortality in order to marry Aragorn.

The other occasion which the Valar clearly do not, perhaps cannot, manage by themselves is the invasion of Valinor by rebellious Númenoreans demanding immortality. Then ". . . the Valar laid down their Guardianship and called upon the One . . ." who sank Númenor under the waves. These incidents serve to show that while the Valar have what Tolkien calls incomprehensibly great "demiurgic" powers, which they use in governing and guarding the affairs of Middle-earth and which justify the invocation of their help in prayer by many of its folk, they are only agents of "the One" and defer to his direct intervention in major emergencies. Beyond this point Tolkien does not choose to go in defining the relationship of the Valar to their superior. Why should he? He has told us all he needs to for the literary-philosophical framework of his tale.

As the Fourth Age begins, no successor of Sauron is in sight to rally the forces of evil against civilization. But signs are not lacking that sooner or later one will arise again on Middle-earth or out of the Undying Lands—another Morgoth, a more vicious Fëanor, a Denethor more wholly lost to good. Gandalf has said as much in the Last Debate: "Other evils there are that may come; for Sauron is himself but a servant or emissary. Yet it is not our part to master all the tides of the world, but to do what is in us for the succour of those years in which we are set, uprooting the evils in the fields that we know, so that those who live after may have clear earth to till. What weather they shall have is not ours to rule." To judge by the history of the past three Ages evil will not be long in reviving. With brief respites Middle-earth has always been under siege by some Dark Lord or other. There seems to be something in the nature of things, or in the nature of the One who devises them, that requires it. Sauron is Morgoth's servant, but whose emissary is Morgoth? In one sense, nobody's. Since like everybody else, he has a will free to choose, he is self-corrupted. In another sense, his master can only be the One, who, while not creating evil, permits it to exist and uses it in ruling his world—who, in truth, *needs* evil in order to bring on times of peril that test his creatures to the uttermost, morally and physically, as in Sauron's war.

If men and their colleagues of other races are to prove the stoutness of their fiber, such times must come again and again in the Fourth Age and future ages of whatever number. Evil has built-in weaknesses that make for self-defeat, and the One, with his smiling ironies, will sometimes manipulate it to that end. But the burden of *The Lord of the Rings* is that victory for the good is never automatic. It must be earned anew each time by every individual taking part. In this effort, says Aragorn to Éomer, man has the natural ability and the obligation to "discern" the difference between right and wrong. These are opposites, absolutes that do not vary from year to year or place to place or people to people. Those rational beings who would act well on Tolkien's Middle-earth do not have to stand on the shifting sands of historical relativism. The good is as unchanging above the tides of time as the beauty of Sam's star over Mordor, and derives ultimately from the character of the One who placed it there.

But does death end all for those who have not the unending lives of elves? The epic abounds with hints of some kind of afterlife for them, but these are faint. For example, the dying Aragorn, when taking leave of Arwen, encourages her to believe that they will meet again: "Behold! we are not bound for ever to the circles of the world, and beyond them is more than memory." But neither he nor anyone else speculates on the question of whether the rewards of virtue extend beyond death. There is plenty of natural religion in *The Lord of the Rings* but the epic tends to stand back from transcendence on this point, as some of Tolkien's shorter tales do not.

The farthest look into the future of mankind on earth is taken by Legolas and Gimli when they first enter Minas Tirith and see the marks of decay around them. The dwarf comments that all the works of men, however promising at first, "fail of their promise." Legolas counters that, even so, "seldom do they fail of their seed," which springs up afresh in unlooked-for times and places to outlast both elves and dwarves. Gimli is unconvinced. Human deeds, he still thinks, "come to naught in the end but might-have-beens." The elf takes refuge in a plea of ignorance: "To that the Elves know not the answer"—and presumably if not the elves, then nobody.

This sad little fugue about the outlook for humanity by representatives of two neighbor races is uncharacteristic in its sadness of the epic as a whole. *The Lord of the Rings* is at bottom a hopeful tale. The whole venture of the Ring always looks desperate. So does combat after combat against wildly superior armies. Yet against all persuasions to despair, Gandalf, Aragorn, Elrond, Faramir, and those who fight beside them hope on and keep on acting upon their hope. Without that, Sauron would have won a dozen times over. Tolkien himself is pessimistic about many aspects of our present age, but he is personally too robust to give up on man. I find the same stoutheartedness in the epic in the teeth of tragedy acknowledged and faced down. It strikes me rather as being a paean to hope.

ROGER SALE

Tolkien and Frodo Baggins

With Tolkien we are back to the cataclysm of World War I, though his reply to the war was different from Lawrence's and was long delayed in taking its crucial shape. Tolkien was born in 1892, so that, though he was only seven years younger than Lawrence, he was still in college when the war started. His experience of the war, while much more immediate than Lawrence's, seems to have been essentially a schoolboy's experience, as Lawrence's certainly was not. Tolkien had been orphaned in 1910 while a student at King Edward's School. He then went to Exeter College, Oxford, from which he was graduated in 1915, just in time, as it were, to join the Lancashire Fusiliers and serve in the trenches around Baupame, where there were very heavy casualties. When the war was over and Tolkien was recovering in a hospital bed in England, he discovered he had only one friend left alive. He has never said much about his wartime experience or his life—the best available information can be found in William Ready's *The Tolkien Relation* (1968) and Henry Resnick's article in *The Saturday Evening Post* for July 2, 1966—but we can gather that in its external details Tolkien's life in wartime France resembled that described by Robert Graves in *Goodbye to All That*. But he said one thing later that seems to me crucial for an understanding of what happened and what kind of man he is: "A real taste for fairy-stories was wakened by philology on the threshold of manhood, and

From *Modern Heroism: Essays on D. H. Lawrence, William Empson, & J. R. R. Tolkien* by Roger Sale. © 1973 by The Regents of the University of California.

quickened to full life by war." It is not an easy sentence to understand, but it has long seemed to me that no one need pursue his inquiry into Tolkien's life any further than he needs to do in order to understand it.

The sentence itself was not written until 1938, and it may well be that it took Tolkien a full twenty years to realize what had happened to him. He seems to have withdrawn from the wounds and terrors of the war and all we think of as modern life. First, and as a prior condition to everything else, he became that most withdrawn of citizens, a philologist—he was an assistant on the revision of the *Oxford English Dictionary*, reader and then professor of philology at Reading, a fellow of Pembroke College, Oxford, and finally Merton Professor of English Literature there—which means that when Tolkien became a writer of fairy tales he was reflecting or expressing his deep absorption in words and older languages. In some sense withdrawing is integral to the life of a philologist, and it is doubtful if very many have ever become philologists without a need to withdraw or flee. He finds, and makes, orders, symbols, systems, traditions he can nurture so they in turn can nourish him. The lore, myth, and magic that surround ancient words can easily be made into a fortress against the modern world, where there is only tumid apathy with no concentration, men and bits of paper.

In *The Tolkien Relation* William Ready offers a portrait of Tolkien in the twenties and thirties which he compiled from the comments of former students and colleagues. As a lecturer, Tolkien's great virtue was as an enunciator of *Beowulf*; as a tutor his strength lay in giving his students ideas he never claimed title to himself; as a scholar his only serious published work before 1936 is an edition of *Sir Gawain and the Green Knight*. He seems, thus, to have been devising ways of living such that he could carry on his relations with the outside world at one remove. What he was, or knew, or cared for, could not be discerned directly, and no one except friends and close admirers need have had any sense of him other than as the figure he obviously offered, of a diffident and learned professor. Nothing that we can see about his life before 1936, at any rate, gives a clue to what he meant when he said, two years later, that his love of fairy tales had been quickened to full life by war.

But beginning in 1936 Tolkien began to show the world some of the fruit of his years of withdrawal. Within two years he delivered his Israel Gollancz Lecture on *Beowulf* to the British Academy, his Andrew Lang Lecture on fairy stories, and published the book he had been reading to his son, *The Hobbit*. Each one of these gives us a different hint of what Tolkien had been doing all those years and of the great work to come. "*Beowulf*: The Monsters and the Critics," which has since become the single best known essay on Old English literature, begins with an attack on philologists and historians who treat the poem as a quarry for their own specialized interests and so ignore the poem itself and the central fact of its monsters. *Beowulf*, he insists, is a poem about war, and we praise Beowulf for fighting long and bravely, though inevitably he will lose in the end. For Tolkien the poem is as much elegy as epic, and thus no Christian overlay, no mention of God or heaven, is strong enough to dispel the sense that the main task of the *scop* is to lament the death of the fallen hero. He superbly evokes the dimly lit and struggling world of Beowulf and Hrothgar, the imminence of Grendel, the inevitability of the dragon's coming, the sternness of the poet's wisdom, and as he does so he makes clear that we can never say of him that he is only a philologist. He speaks as one immersed in the lore and the atmosphere of old Germanic things, as one who has not just withdrawn from the modern world but gone somewhere else as well.

At first glance *The Hobbit* seems worlds removed from *Beowulf* and Tolkien's meditation on it. Like *The Wind in the Willows* and the Pooh books, which were also written by upper-middle-class Englishmen to read aloud to their sons, *The Hobbit* is episodic and cozy, anything but stern and austere. It begins this way:

> In a hole in the ground there lived a hobbit. Not a nasty, dirty, wet hole, filled with the ends of worms and an oozy smell, nor yet a dry, bare, sandy hole with nothing in it to sit down on or to eat: it was a hobbit-hole, and that means comfort.

Though the hobbit-hole may seem far away from Hrothgar's mead hall, in fact it takes little effort to get from one to the other. All that is required is the mastery of two different tones, both of which are distinctly literary and distinctly not modern. The author of both the lecture and the children's book is very obviously a reader about things long past, an imaginer of worlds free of the strain or despair of the modernist, worlds of lore and wonder where names can evoke magical things. *The Hobbit* goes on:

> I suppose hobbits need some description nowadays, since they have become rare and shy of the Big People, as they call us. They are (or were) small people, smaller than dwarves (and they have no beards) but very much larger than lilliputians. There is little or no magic about them, except the ordinary everyday sort which helps them to disappear quietly and quickly when large stupid folk like you and me come blundering along, making a noise like elephants which they can hear a mile off.

Tolkien is instructing his son from a position similar to that he takes to
instruct his audience in the *Beowulf* lecture. In each case he allies himself with
his audience against some outsiders: "critics" they are called in the lecture,
and "Big People" in the book, but they are obviously the same sort in each
case. It is only the resolutely Anglophilic who like the voice of *The Hobbit*;
others tend to find it too cozy and seemingly smug. The hobbits are
recognizable English types, fond of beer and tobacco and good conversation,
easily able to live without the restraints of police or women. C. S. Lewis's
descriptions of the Inklings, the Oxford group that included Tolkien, Charles
Williams, himself, and a few others, seem descriptive of hobbit life. Though
the book is subtitled "There and Back Again," though there are adventures
and dwarves and a magic ring, it is a static book; things happen but change
is not possible.

The Hobbit is often taken to be a good introduction to Tolkien's major
work, because it too is about hobbits, but if *The Lord of the Rings* needs any
introduction at all, the Andrew Lang Lecture, "On Fairy-Stories," which
Tolkien gave in 1938, provides the best. It is here he says that his love of fairy
tales was quickened to full life by war, though he does not really explain the
sentence. I am going to look at some parts of the lecture more closely later
on; for now it is enough to say that here Tolkien describes what men in later
days lost when they left behind the world created in fairy stories, and which
we can begin to recover primarily through such stories. Fairy stories let us
see or discover the world as we originally were meant to see it. We are left to
imagine that the stupidity, barbarity, squalor, and horror of the war drove a
sensitive young imagination toward the conviction that he was seeing the
very opposite of life as it was meant to be seen. The horrors of World War I
were trite, those of fairy tale brilliant and profound. Again we see that while
withdrawal may have been a psychic necessity for Tolkien he made of it not
just a journey away but a journey toward. Ironically, and wonderfully, as we
will see, it was by means of his withdrawal and his imagining of a fairy tale
that Tolkien could create one of the most powerful visions we have of the
very world from which he was fleeing.

At about the same time, Tolkien was beginning this work to which the
years of withdrawal and the slow flowering of scholarship and tale-telling had
led him, though it was years before it was finished and published. For what
he wanted to do, it seems, the scholarship on *Beowulf* and *Gawain* was too
limited or too impersonal, the atmosphere of *The Hobbit* too confining, the
point of "On Fairy-Stories" too doctrinal. His is a more capacious and
inquiring imagination than perhaps anyone, including Tolkien himself, could
have guessed in the late thirties. In any event, long after the modern age had
passed and not only the first but the second war was over and Tolkien himself

was near retirement, there appeared at yearly intervals the three volumes of *The Lord of the Rings*: *The Fellowship of the Ring* (1954), *The Two Towers* (1955), *The Return of the King* (1956).

As I have said, some people like to use some of Tolkien's early work as an introduction to the trilogy, just as some people begin reading Spenser with *The Shepheardes Calender* and Milton with the Nativity Ode, but the game is not really worth the candle. As we read the trilogy we can be reminded of this or that aspect of his other work, we are aware that he is an English don, a philologist, a writer in love with lore and naming, but all this is the soil of Tolkien's imagination, not the fruit. Tolkien needed his years of withdrawal, but not so he could glorify some way of life so long forgotten that it can be recalled only by the most nostalgic. When Tolkien says he wished he could have written the trilogy in Elvish, he is declaring his temperamental allegiance to the distant past, but the imagination plays strange tricks, seldom more strikingly than in *The Lord of the Rings*. Tolkien tries in many different ways to bring ancient values to life, but by and large he fails to do so. Neither his learning nor his fear of modern life could alter the fact that he is of the modern world, better able to render his own century imaginatively than any other. Technically the central action of *The Lord of the Rings* is a quest, and we know quite well that there are no modern quests, but in fact the central action more closely resembles a descent into hell. Tolkien could not have done this without displacing his story into the fairyland of Middle Earth, without using many ritual details of quest literature, but that does not change in any significant way the fact that at its best the trilogy is modern literature.

To say this, and to insist upon it as I will be doing, is bound to seem at least a little impertinent to Tolkien himself who might not understand this point and who, if he did, would not like it. But *The Lord of the Rings* is what it is, a superb instance of the rightness of Lawrence's statement that we must trust the tale and not the artist. I have called this chapter "Tolkien and Frodo Baggins," and in a number of places I speak of Frodo almost as though he were a free agent, separate and equal to Tolkien. I do this, in the first place, because it is Frodo's heroism that is clearly visible to us and is our guide to see and understand Tolkien's heroism, which is not on view in the way Lawrence's or Empson's is. But second and more important, I do this as a way of stressing that Frodo is, unlike a great deal else in the trilogy, modern, and that as a result it is to Frodo that Tolkien's imagination responds most fully, with or without his conscious knowledge. Because this may be true without Tolkien's having been aware of it, it is difficult to talk of his heroism, but the work makes clear that he is heroic. It is as though Tolkien's imagination rescues him from his convictions, and our best sign of this is the way the buttons tell the truth: Frodo Lives. The buttons probably mean that Frodo is alive and well in Argentina, and I mean that Frodo, and the figures nearest him, Sam Gamgee and Gollum, live as the major justification of the whole work, and that the work itself never makes this clear.

Justice cannot be done to Frodo's heroism or to the ways it is the key to Tolkien's heroism by treating Frodo alone. He has a context, and it is his gradual emergence from that context that makes him seem different and so impressive. We must begin by returning to the hobbits and to the way they fit into the fabric of Tolkien's imagination. In *The Hobbit* Tolkien is generally content to remain complacent about the hobbits' own complacency and lore, while in *The Lord of the Rings* he generally understands (for what it is) their desire to withdraw from any world more complex than a daydream—and so is able to place them critically. Occasionally Tolkien relaxes with the hobbits and pretends that buffoonery and schoolboy pluck are important responses to danger, but these lapses are infrequent and easily identified. The real issue at stake here is much larger than the hobbits' coziness, and that is Tolkien's love of lore, his endless naming, his ritual details, those qualities that are Tolkien's way of withdrawing and of making a world that is an adaptation of many older worlds. Tolkien will include anything as long as it bears no touch of the modern. The hobbits' names—Baggins, Sackville, Proudfoot, Gamgee, Took, Cotton—all are versions of names Tolkien might have found in a parish register in Buckinghamshire; their home is called The Shire. But we need a passage, and one about war rather than hobbits, to see how Tolkien uses his names to include many old things that are clearly not of our century:

> But everywhere he looked he saw the signs of war. The Misty Mountains were crawling like anthills: orcs were issuing out of a thousand holes. Under the boughs of Mirkwood there was deadly strife of Elves and Men and fell beasts. The land of the Beornings was aflame; a cloud was over Moria; smoke rose on the borders of Lórien.
>
> Horsemen were galloping on the grass of Rohan; wolves poured from Isengard. From the havens of Harad ships of war put out to sea; and out of the East Men were moving endlessly: swordsmen, spearmen, bowmen upon horses, chariots of chieftains and laden wains. All the power of the Dark Lord was in motion.

Anyone who finds this too stiff and pretentious probably will not be able to read *The Lord of the Rings* with much pleasure. This is not Tolkien at his best, but it is characteristic. The reference to chariots, chieftains, and wains in the next-to-last sentence self-consciously places us in a preindustrial scene, and all the military details show that this is ancient, or at least old-fashioned, warfare, anything but the trenches of France. The names are also self-consciously chosen to convey a sense of scope and variety: Misty Mountains and Mirkwood are children's book names; elves and orcs come from fairy stories; Moria, like the country of the Dark Lord, Mordor, derives from Mordred, the faithless among Arthur's knights; Lórien, the forest of the elves, is one of a series of "L" words Tolkien uses to connote good, elvish things—its king and queen are Celeborn and Galadriel; Isengard combines the Old English *isen* and *geard* to form the kenning "iron-castle"; Harad is close to Arabic and so names a place far away from the main action. A full Tolkien entymology has not yet been done, so far as I know, but even a casual student of older English and northern literature will recognize over and over again sounds and combinations of sounds that show Tolkien adapting his names from earlier ones. The purpose is not to provide a riddle or a code, or to encourage a reader to feel he must be more learned in order to understand, but to evoke a world we know has long since passed away where naming is taken to be a matter of grave importance and where, therefore, all names are appropriate. An interest in names and the past they evoke is one major sign of the goodness of the "good" characters, just as evil is the effort to alter or destroy the right relation of namer to named, present to past.

This is the essential withdrawn Tolkien, and, as I have said, this is the soil of his imagination. We must now turn to his central story and myth, that of the Ring, to see how it transformed an important part of that imagination. In *The Hobbit* the Ring is just a ring, and part of just one more episode. Bilbo Baggins finds it in an underground tunnel near a dark lake, and he also meets there a slimy creature called Gollum who, it becomes clear, owned the ring and used it to make himself invisible so he could catch goblins. Gollum discovers his loss, suspects Bilbo has found the ring, and Bilbo discovers the ring's power to make him invisible just in time to escape. There is nothing in the episode to lead anyone to suspect what was going to happen. Shortly after he finished *The Hobbit* Tolkien began the trilogy, which could not have been written without Bilbo's acquisition having assumed major proportions in Tolkien's imagination. At the opening of *The Fellowship of the Ring*, Bilbo is planning to leave his home in The Shire, and he reluctantly leaves the ring for his nephew and heir, Frodo Baggins, who knows about it only through Bilbo's story of how he found it. Later Frodo is visited by an old friend of Bilbo's, a wizard named Gandalf, who tells him that his ring is The Ring, forged by Sauron, the Dark Lord, as a master ring, one that could bind and control all the rings of power that had been fashioned in an earlier age by the elves for themselves, dwarves, and men. Sauron lost the Ring in an earlier war, and by a series of accidents it came into the hands of Sméagol, or Gollum, one of some hobbit-like creatures that lived near the River Anduin, into which the Ring had fallen. Gandalf then shows Frodo the inscription on the Ring, which is the sixth and seventh lines of this poem, long known to the elves:

> Three Rings for the Elven-kings under the sky,
>   Seven for the Dwarf-lords in their halls of stone,
> Nine for Mortal Men doomed to die,
>   One for the Dark Lord on his dark throne
> In the Land of Mordor where the Shadows lie.
>   One Ring to rule them all, One Ring to find them,
>   One Ring to bring them all and in the darkness bind them
> In the Land of Mordor where the Shadows lie.

In a work filled with riddles, songs, and lays, this is the only poem about the Ring, and it is much the best and most important of the lot. Here, at the beginning, it mystifies both Frodo and the reader at least as much as it explains. Gandalf can tell Frodo about the three elven rings and the seven dwarf rings, but Frodo's response to such lore is not unlike ours: I have heard of such, but not in my world. Gandalf then tells Frodo that the Dark Lord, Sauron, has risen again in Mordor, and that he has gradually pieced together the history of the Ring and is at that moment known to be searching for a hobbit by the name of Baggins. Frodo asks Gandalf why they do not just destroy the Ring, and Gandalf tells him to try:

> It was an admirable thing and altogether precious. When he took it out he had intended to fling it from him into the very hottest part of the fire. But he found now that he could not do so, not without a great struggle. He weighed the Ring in his hand, hesitating, and forcing himself to remember all that Gandalf had told him; and then with an effort of will he made a movement, as if to cast it away—but he found that he had put it back in his pocket.

Frodo begins to understand, and also to see he is being asked to undertake something he feels is beyond him:

> "You are wise and powerful. Will you not take the Ring?"
> "No!" cried Gandalf, springing to his feet. "With that power I should have power too great and terrible. And over me the Ring would gain a power still greater and more deadly."

The Ring's only use is to bind and subdue others, just as here it has bound Frodo to the extent that he cannot choose to throw it in the fire. As it turns out, it would have made no difference had he done so, because the Ring would remain untouched. It can be destroyed only in the fire in which it was forged, on Mount Orodruin or Mount Doom, in the land of Mordor, home of Sauron, where the Shadows lie.

The idea of the Ring is really quite simple, and though it is not until much later that its ramifications become clearer and its power can be fully felt, even this early it is clear that the idea of the Ring can do much for Tolkien. The stronger the Ring-bearer the stronger his temptation to use the Ring himself and so be bound by it. This means that Tolkien can employ many of the traditional figures of fairy tales like wizards, dwarves, and elves, and can work to make them as impressive and powerful as he likes, but that they must always be a little irrelevant because Frodo, neither impressive nor powerful, is Ring-bearer at the moment, and is at least as able to accomplish its destruction as anyone else, even though he has no credentials as a hero whatsoever. No one is suited for this perilous quest. Frodo knows about dwarves and elves and the rest exactly what we know—what we have been told or read about—and suddenly he is asked to leave home and find out about all this for himself. He has no recourse but to see it as "adventure" even though he can read in Gandalf's tone a sense that much more is involved than he understands. The myth of the Ring gives Tolkien a double perspective, in this scene that of Gandalf and Frodo, lore-knower and bemused troubled innocent, and at the same time lets him show that the latter is at least as important as the former. In a poem that is at first glance as far removed from Tolkien as seems possible, Dr. Johnson asks: "What murdered Wentworth, and what exiled Hyde?" The answer is: "Power too great to keep, or to resign," which is precisely Gandalf's answer to Frodo's questions about destroying the Ring or giving it to someone more powerful than himself. It will take heroism of some kind, though of what kind no one can glimpse this early in the trilogy, to hold onto the Ring, to take it to Mordor, to give it up there, and thereby to avoid the fate of Wentworth, Hyde, and the fate Gandalf foresees for himself were he ever to have the Ring.

So Frodo sells his house and sends out word he is retiring to the home of his childhood, farther east in The Shire. Even before he leaves he learns he must hurry, because mysterious Black Riders who look like men come into The Shire and ask after a hobbit named Baggins. Frodo leaves stealthily, keeping away from the high road when he can, accompanied by his servant, Sam Gamgee, and the young hobbits, Pippin Took, and, later, Merry

Brandybuck. All the other hobbits know is that Frodo is in danger and must go on a long journey, and Frodo himself knows little more. Gandalf has advised them to head eastward to Rivendell, the home of Elrond Halfelven. A group of friendly elves appears, then an eccentric named Tom Bombadil in an ancient forest, then barrow-wights, more Black Riders, then a Ranger named Strider who rescues them in a pub in the town of Bree after Frodo has given himself away by letting the Ring slip on his finger during a tavern show so that he becomes invisible. Through all these early chapters Tolkien moves deliberately, slowly expanding the world of the hobbits. Some readers who start by thinking they will not like Tolkien move through these episodes feeling that this is just a dressing-up of some old and musty story. But as anyone can see when he looks back at these chapters from some later point in the trilogy, Tolkien knows what he is doing. The hobbits are like us in their attitude toward the lore and mysteries of life outside their own province. They move provincially, clumsily, relating everything they see to what they know from life at home, as though their way of understanding the world, no matter how inadequate, was the only one they could possibly have. Thus Tolkien must move slowly, altering landscape and mode little by little, in order to trap the hobbits in their provinciality.

When Frodo becomes invisible in Bree, he reveals the location of the Ring to all the Black Riders, and so the hobbits flee, guided by Strider, moving circuitously now because the highway is constantly watched. Even so the Riders catch up to them one night and Frodo feels compelled to put on the Ring, which makes him invisible to his companions but which reveals his exact location to the Riders, one of whom wounds Frodo badly. Finally, after a dash along the highway, the hobbits, Strider, and an elf carry Frodo to Rivendell. Here Frodo can begin to heal, and here Elrond has called a council—Gandalf, Bilbo, elves, dwarves, and men are there—and the hobbits can begin to see how vast the world is and how much is at stake in their journey with the Ring. The part of the book that feels and reads like "adventures" is over, for them and us.

At the council Glóin, a dwarf, begins by telling of Sauron's efforts to use the dwarf-lord to find Bilbo and so regain the Ring; Elrond describes how the Ring was first taken from Sauron by Isildur; Boromir, a man from Gondor, announces that Sauron has moved out of Mordor to reoccupy land in Gondor taken from him in his last defeat. He also repeats a prophecy he heard in a dream that he could not understand:

> Seek for the Sword that was broken:
>   In Imladris it dwells;
> There shall be counsels taken
>   Stronger than Morgul-spells.

> There shall be shown a token
>   That Doom is near at hand,
> For Isildur's Bane shall waken,
>   And the Halfling forth shall stand.

Strider then stands forth with the "Sword that was broken," and Elrond tells the others that Strider is in fact Aragorn, heir to the kingdom of Gondor. He then introduces Frodo with the Ring, and the halfling stands forth.

Here lore and action meet, but not in a way that either hobbits or readers can readily understand. It does not really tell Frodo anything to learn that the Ring is "Isildur's Bane," and it cannot really matter to him that Strider is Aragorn. Lore is still only names and songs and stories about the past, and all that happens at the council can be significant only to those like Gandalf and Aragorn who already know what the lore signifies. Frodo does not even know what questions to ask that might give him answers to put together the fragments he has learned about. Boromir's prophecy and the rest are for him like the quotations in Eliot's poems for us: they recall something we have heard about but have never really grasped no matter how well we know the words themselves. And when Frodo does learn of something he can understand, as when Gandalf describes how he traced the passing of the Ring from Isildur to Gollum to Bilbo, and Bilbo tells how he later gave it to Frodo, he really only sees more clearly how irrelevant a good deal of it is to what he must do. The war seems to be between Sauron and the members of the council, but a great many there cannot really help Frodo. The elf-lords seem glorious to the hobbits but they are faded now, rulers of small lands, unable and uninterested in stirring abroad. Aragorn and Gandalf can do much more because they have knowledge and power to help show Frodo the way, and as long as he is with them they can forge links between the wisdom of the past and the urgency of the present. Still, Frodo is the Ring-bearer: "I will take the Ring, though I do not know the way." A fellowship is formed to go with him, south with the Ring: the four hobbits, Gandalf, Aragorn, Boromir the man, Legolas the elf, and Gimli the dwarf. But the fact that there is no need for a powerful army because that would only attract attention and an even more powerful army from Sauron, also emphasizes the limitedness of the help anyone can give Frodo. He is best armed, though he does not quite realize it when Gandalf tells him so, by the fact that Sauron will not conceive that anyone could want to destroy the Ring and so will not be looking for them to move toward Mordor.

The fellowship moves through Moria, the ancient underground mountain kingdom of the dwarves, and in a fierce fight there with a Balrog, Gandalf is lost and Aragorn assumes command. The company then moves out of the mountains and into Lothlórien, forest home of the elven-queen

Galadriel, where "All that he [Frodo] saw was shapely, but the shapes seemed at once clear cut, as if they had been first conceived and drawn at the uncovering of his eyes, and ancient as if they had endured for ever." In Moria and Lothlórien the hobbits can begin to see for themselves the ancientness of life that had been, before this, only the lore of others. Once again, in *The Fellowship of the Ring*, as in *The Rainbow* and *Some Versions of Pastoral*, the would-be hero must become a historian first, able to explore the past in order to see its implications for the present.

In Moria the hobbits meet creatures, some merely ferocious and others really malicious, who know and care nothing about the Ring or the perilous journey: wargs, orcs, the Balrog. At one point Boromir casually throws a stone into a pool, and Frodo says: "I am afraid of the pool. Don't disturb it!" One can "disturb" the water of a pool by throwing a stone, but that is nothing to be afraid of. Frodo is beginning to sense, however, that the world is alive in many and dangerous ways, and he is right: "Out from the water a long sinuous tentacle had crawled; it was pale-green and luminous and wet." In Lothlórien there is respite from struggle and danger, and also discovery:

> In Rivendell there was memory of ancient things; in Lórien the ancient things still lived on in the waking world. Evil had been seen and heard there, sorrow had been known; the Elves feared and distrusted the world outside: wolves were howling on the wood's borders: but on the land of Lórien no shadow lay.

The rampant and threatening vitality of Moria, the preserved stillness of Lothlórien—"In winter here no heart could mourn for summer or for spring"—in one sense we are only passing through places on the way south, but these are anything but mere episodes because we begin to see what the journey is all about. The hobbits have no way to understand Gandalf at the beginning when he says The Shire is in danger, and in Rivendell they are so overwhelmed by the "memory of ancient things," they can only glimpse any relation between what had happened and what is happening. But in Moria an ancient kingdom had fallen—there are enchanted doors and winding stairs and great halls still left to remind—and what remains is unordered, fierce, not quite a chaos but almost. In Lothlórien another such kingdom is fading, and gradually Frodo and we see that these words, these civilizations, simply are following their natural course, rising and falling in the flux of history. The more clearly this is felt and understood, the more important the present becomes because if Sauron regains the Ring the whole process of history will be his to control. The Ring seeks and binds, and in binding it aborts process.

Quite unlike Sauron, the Balrog in Moria fights and terrorizes the fellowship
when he feels his territory is invaded; there is nothing friendly or good about
him, but he is not evil. To be alive, Balrog or dwarf or elf, is to follow one's
own nature, whatever that be. To be bound is to have the part of oneself that
is unique destroyed. Just as lore is the means whereby sentient and articulate
creatures assert and nourish their uniqueness by keeping their ties with the
past, so war is the struggle to be alive fought against any who seek to destroy
lore and the relations it implies.

Such a formulation is not made by Tolkien or any hobbit, but it can
help to show how the trilogy reveals its subject. The word "natural," for
instance, is unknown in *The Lord of the Rings*, but passages like the following
make the word seem appropriate:

> "There lies the fastness of Southern Mirkwood," said
> Haldir. "It is clad in a forest of dark fir, where the trees strive one
> against another and their branches rot and wither. In the midst
> upon a stony height stands Dol Goldur, where long the hidden
> Enemy had his dwelling. We fear that now it is inhabited again,
> and with power sevenfold. A black cloud lies often over it of late.
> In this high place you may see the two powers that are opposed
> one to another; and ever they strive now in thought, but whereas
> the light perceives the very heart of the darkness, its own secret
> has not been discovered. Not yet."

This is stiff and ancient, but the magic is at work in it, too. Tolkien here
repeats a verb, "strive," so that the subjects and objects moved by the verb
make a kind of metaphor: the trees in the forest of Mirkwood "strive," and
then the two powers "strive." Just as tree against tree leads to rotting and
withering, so too light against dark leads to war. We know, or sense, that the
trees are "real" trees, whereas the light and the dark powers are symbolic, but
the effect of the comparison is to make us think of the ways the symbolic
powers are behaving naturally, like the trees, and indeed, we recognize, rays
of light do "perceive" darkness.

But "light," though "real" and "natural," does symbolize the moral
power of goodness, or, rather, can describe and even explain what that power
is:

> At the hill's foot Frodo found Aragorn, standing still and
> *silent as a tree*; but in his hand was a small golden bloom of
> *elanor*, and a *light was in his eyes*. He was *wrapped in some fair
> memory*: and as Frodo looked at him he knew that he beheld

things as they once had been in this same place. For the *grim years were removed* from the face of Aragorn, and he seemed clothed in white, a young lord tall and fair; and he spoke words in the Elvish tongue to one whom Frodo could not see. [italics (except "elanor") mine]

This is a stunning passage, but it demands the context of the whole work to this point to make it so. The italicized phrases all might be spotted as clichés if we were not forced to take them literally as well as metaphorically. In Lothlórien, for that is the point about it, the trees are now silent but once were not, so that the phrase "silent as a tree" does not mean, simply, "quiet," but something much closer to "deliberately silent." The light from Lothlórien shines from a vanished world, and the light that Aragorn once saw when the forest was alive now shines only as a memory. Yet because Aragorn can remember he can be wrapped in that memory and the light in his eyes thus does what lore is usually employed to do—it illuminates the present by remembering the past. All this is clinched with a simple and lovely ambiguity: in "as Frodo looked at him he knew that he beheld things as they once had been," the second "he" refers to Aragorn or to Frodo, and so to both. The light that wraps Aragorn in memory is seen by Frodo in Aragorn's eyes, and Frodo understands a historical relation as he never has before.

Thus "light" becomes not just natural force or a cliché for moral power, but also is descriptive of the historical "natural" motion of living things. Because Frodo is there to see and to discover the past, Aragorn's transformation into a "young lord tall and fair" is not the literary or fey magic of a teller of fairy tales, but the "real" or "natural" magic of seeing the present clearly and rightly because the past is, for the first time, clearly and rightly seen. The war, thus, is not just a struggle between the moral forces of good and evil, light and dark, but a fight to be "natural" and unbound when life is threatened. The "One Ring to bring them all and in the darkness bind them" now seems less an idea with which to animate a tale and more a threat to living things.

After leaving Lothlórien the fellowship moves south down the River Anduin, the boundary, much farther south, between Mordor and Gondor. Boromir tries to persuade Frodo to go with him to Gondor, but Frodo knows he must go straight to Mordor because there is nothing in Gondor or any place else that he can help or that can help him. Boromir has no way of knowing, because to him the Ring is just magic, Isildur's Bane, what Frodo increasingly is discovering, the awful and heavy burden of bearing the Ring, and so he thinks the Ring can and should be used like a weapon in the coming war. When Frodo insistently refuses, Boromir tries to force the Ring from him, and Frodo can escape only by putting on the Ring and disappearing across the river. Only his servant, Sam Gamgee, figures out what has happened and so follows him, while the others remain on the west bank and find themselves attacked by a band of orcs. The fellowship thus is broken, and the first volume ends.

It is a very good book, *The Fellowship of the Ring*, the one that most improves with each rereading. There are slow places near the beginning—Bilbo's birthday party, the first meeting with the elves, especially the long interlude with Tom Bombadil—and, furthermore, nothing in it matches the best things in the next two volumes. But Tolkien has great limitations as a writer about battles and the heroism they demand, and much of the last two volumes is about battles. As a writer about danger, however, Tolkien hardly has an equal, and in *The Fellowship of the Ring* he often wonderfully shows how a world that is expanding and becoming more resonant and understandable is at the same time becoming more dangerous. At the beginning, for instance, we have the Black Riders, who are like villains in children's books; we accept them literarily and so do not in the least feel endangered by them. By the end of *The Fellowship of the Ring*, however, though the Black Riders have not changed, our view and Frodo's view of them have, because we know so much more about the power of the Ring. Thus Tolkien's naming of them must change too, and they are no longer the Black Riders but the Nazgûl, the Ringwraiths, the nine mortal men doomed to die, wraiths and doomed because bound, because cut off from other men, without lore or any vital relation between present and past, the very definition of shadow: "a dark shape, like a cloud and yet not a cloud, for it moved far more swiftly, came out of the blackness in the South, and sped towards the Company, blotting out all light as it approached." Frodo has not only learned about the Riders and been wounded by one of them but also has learned a great deal about light in Lothlórien, and so: "Frodo felt a sudden chill running through him and clutching at his heart; there was a deadly cold, like the memory of an old wound, in his shoulder. He crouched down, as if to hide." There is no sense of heroism or of any possible adventure here. What it means to bear the Ring, to become more bound to it, is becoming clearer in the very process of its being felt as a chill and a terror from which one wishes to hide.

In the next two volumes Tolkien splits his narrative. The first part of each describes the coming of the war to the lands west of the Anduin—to the forest of Fangorn, the plains of Rohan and Helm's Deep, Saruman's castle Isengard, and finally Gondor—as it happens to the members of the fellowship left on the west bank of the river: Aragorn, Merry, Pippin, Legolas, Gimli, and Gandalf who returns from his fight with the Balrog. The second half of each volume covers the trip of Frodo and Sam to Mordor. This journey, where the trilogy reaches its greatest heights, is vastly superior in quality to the story of the war in the west, and for reasons that allow us to see why of all the kinds of heroism the war entails, only the modern heroism of Frodo really strikes resonant chords in Tolkien's imagination. As Frodo becomes heroic, so too does Tolkien; both, as it were, cast off all trace of the mustiness of the lore and the snugness of the living in The Shire, and move into the present and face it heroically.

I have tried to indicate how much of Tolkien's success depends on the hobbits, and on the perspective he gives them, and us. The story of the Ring shows what everything in Tolkien's Middle Earth is all about, but that story only gains its full force when "shows" means "shows a hobbit." As a simple matter of arranging words, Tolkien can make the world "live" by taking all the dead metaphors he knows and using them as though they were not dead—"the sun climbed the sky," "the wind fell still," "now a star had descended into the very earth"—it is an easy enough device. But, as we have seen in the passages where Frodo sees Aragorn wrapped in memory and the Ringwraith blots out the sun, when a hobbit is there to see and to respond, then the dead metaphor really can come alive. Tolkien himself seems to have understood this only imperfectly. There are times when he magnificently makes the whole tissue of aliveness the whole issue of the war by making one of the hobbits see something freshly, and by making us see a formerly dead metaphor gain great resonance, and Tolkien must have known that our seeing depended on the hobbits' seeing. But there are many times, especially in the last two volumes, when the wind murmurs or the shadow blocks and all we have is ornamental language being manipulated, and Tolkien seems unaware of how tired his writing can seem, how simply literary and old-fashioned, when the language is not his instrument for making someone see how literary and old-fashioned things can reveal the present danger.

There is a doctrinal point that needs to be brought in here. In his Andrew Lang Lecture of 1939, "On Fairy-Stories," Tolkien writes about the importance of having us see the aliveness of the world:

> Recovery (which includes return and renewal of health) is a re-gaining—regaining of a clear view. I do not say "seeing things as they are" and involve myself with the philosophers, though I might venture to say "seeing things as we are (or were) meant to see them"—as things apart from ourselves. We need, in any case, to clean our windows; so that the things seen clearly may be freed from the drab blur of triteness or familiarity—from possessiveness. Of all faces those of our

familiares are the ones both most difficult to play fantastic tricks with, and most difficult really to see with fresh attention, perceiving their likeness and unlikeness: that they are faces, and yet unique faces. This triteness is really the penalty of "appropriation": the things that are trite, or (in a bad sense) familiar, are the things that we have appropriated, legally or mentally. We say we know them. They have become like the things which once attracted us by their glitter, or their colour, or their shape, and we laid hands on them, and then locked them in our hoard, acquired them, and acquiring ceased to look at them.

Tolkien says the essay was written "when *The Lord of the Rings* was beginning to unroll itself and to unfold prospects of labour and exploration in yet unknown country as daunting to me as to the hobbits," and the essay and the trilogy cast revealing lights on each other. I have called this passage doctrinal, and thereby have implied a pejorative point about it, but it would do almost as well simply to say that what is stated here about Recovery is what is enacted in the trilogy by the hobbits, by us if we are willing, and, in ways I do not think Tolkien was aware of, by Tolkien himself.

We "recover" something when we no longer possess it familiarly, when we see with the freshness of our childish seeing. Fairy stories make us see with the freshness our culture had before it too possessed the world around it. The psychological point about ourselves as individuals is true, and in ways we all easily recognize. The point about fairy stories being an important way to recover is something we all perhaps can vaguely assent to, but for Tolkien it is of much graver importance than it is for most of us, because fairy stories, like philology, are his means of locating himself in the past such that he can say about the present that we all live behind dirty windows:

> The incarnate mind, the tongue, and the tale are in our world coeval. The human mind, endowed with the powers of generalization and abstraction, sees not only *green-grass*, discriminating it from other things (and finding it fair to look upon), but sees that it is *green* as well as being *grass*. But how powerful, how stimulating to the very faculty that produced it, was the invention of the adjective: no spell or incantation in Faërie is more potent. And that is not surprising: such incantations might indeed be said to be only another view of adjectives, a part of speech in a mythical grammar. The mind that thought of *light, heavy, grey, yellow, still, swift*, also conceived of magic that would make heavy things light and

able to fly, turn grey lead into yellow gold, and the still rock
into a swift water. If it could do the one, it could do the other;
it inevitably did both. When we can take green from grass, blue
from heaven, and red from blood, we have already an
enchanter's power . . . in such "fantasy," as it is called, new form
is made; Faërie begins; Man becomes a sub-creator.

To write fairy stories, then, is to go back as best one can to the moment when
Faërie began, and *green* was taken from *grass* and put on a man's face to make
a horror. It is to Recover, to see green and grass as though for the first time,
to write about them as though just discovering the power of words, to know
how things were meant to be seen.

It is not difficult to imagine that the acquisition of this idea of Recovery
was a very important step in Tolkien's development. Anyone who has worked
at all with old languages or older forms of our own language knows that at
certain moments a word can convey the sense that that word was made so we
could know how something was meant to be seen: the Mediterranean really
is wine-dark, the North Sea hrim-cald. At those points in our civilization
men took an especial care in seeing and naming what was important: sea, sky,
tree, sword, king. To become a student of those words and the historical
periods in which they were made is almost always to become convinced that
we in our own time have lost that care. For Tolkien the doctrine of Recovery
was justification for his withdrawal, because it meant that he was not just
leaving but going, and finding. To be able to see in the study of words and,
eventually, in the writing of fairy stories, a way away from the ravages and
complications of a world that seems mostly proud of its capacity to make
gadgets and complicated social organizations is to give an almost religious
basis to the Myth of Lost Unity. When he gained his sense of Recovery, of
seeing things as they were meant to be seen, Tolkien found what George
Eliot's Mr. Casaubon could not find, a key to all mythologies, and Tolkien
was no longer withdrawn because defeated but withdrawn because finding.

Tolkien could at this point have been content merely to relax, to use his
idea of Recovery as a fortress behind which he could then have proceeded to
invent, to spin out words and worlds, to be elvish. He could also have done
what C. S. Lewis did, to stand up behind one of the turrets on the fortress
and inform the world outside of all it was missing. When Tolkien says that
hobbits are still around but we Big People cannot see them because we make
too much noise, he is being both relaxed and preachy, as he is in some
stretches of the last two volumes we will look at later. But for Tolkien the idea
is not just an idea, or a dogma; it is enacted. In *The Hobbit* this is not yet the
case. When Bilbo Baggins leaves The Shire he has "adventures," he learns

the lore of dwarves and elves and dragons as lore, and Recovers nothing. But in *The Fellowship of the Ring* this acceptance of the familiar as natural and the unfamiliar as adventurous is precisely what Frodo must stop doing. So too Tolkien forces his reader to give up his sense that he knows all about Middle Earth because he has read Kenneth Grahame and Beatrix Potter and has heard of dwarves and elves and thinks he knows what kind of book has such creatures in them. The hobbits are possessive of their world—they bind it to themselves—at the beginning, just as we are possessive about books with hobbits, and both we and the hobbits are made free by the story of the Ring "from the drab blur of triteness or familiarity." Among the hobbits, Frodo is much more strongly forced into this new seeing because he carries and is increasingly burdened by the Ring that embodies the final possessiveness, the ultimate power to bind things apart from ourselves to ourselves. Sauron's weakness is precisely that he is bound by the Ring and so he cannot imagine others seeing the world differently than he does—"That we should try to destroy the Ring itself has not yet entered into his darkest dream," says Gandalf.

What is most striking here is recognizing what this imagining did for Tolkien himself. Tolkien is not the first to have an idea of Recovery, but almost all the others who formulated such or similar ideas continued to see the present, the world of their own life, tritely, possessively. So much in the idea tempts one to be backward-looking—that is not its point, one presumes, but it must have seemed so to many—and seems to offer a way to withdraw from the present and go back into the vision of one's childhood and the life of the early years of the civilization. And Tolkien, when speaking in his own voice, can indeed be very trite and unseeing about the twentieth century:

> Not long ago—incredible though it may seem—I heard a clerk of Oxenford declare that he "welcomed" the proximity of mass-production robot factories, and the roar of self-obstructive mechanical traffic, because it brought his university into "contact with real life." He may have meant that the way men were living and working in the twentieth century was increasing in barbarity at an alarming rate, and that the loud demonstration of this in the streets of Oxford might serve as a warning that it is not possible to preserve for long an oasis of sanity in a desert of unreason by mere fences, without actual offensive action (practical and intellectual). I fear he did not. In any case the expression "real life" in this context seems to fall short of academic standards. The notion that motor-cars are more "alive" than, say, centaurs or dragons is curious; that they

are more "real" than, say, horses, is pathetically absurd. How real, how startlingly alive is a factory chimney compared with an elm-tree: poor obsolete thing, insubstantial dream of an escapist!

And he ends another paragraph of comparing various things mechanical with various things "natural" with "Fairy-stories might be, I guess, better Masters of Arts than the academic person I have referred to."

But there is no need to trust the artist when we can trust the tale. Tolkien's vision of modern life in the second and third volumes of the trilogy will not be precisely that of a Lawrence or a Joyce, but it need not be, and it very definitely is modern life that Tolkien is envisioning here, and Recovering as well. Supported by his immense learning of Old things, emboldened by the idea that we can clean our windows and see freshly, Tolkien was thereby enabled to do what no one else, so far as I know, who shared or shares his beliefs was able to do: come back to the present, face the very things that had made him withdraw in the first place. To make a hobbit see the vitality and irrelevance of the past and the immensity of the world and of the Dark Lord's desire to possess it, is to see oneself in the present anew, and to be a modern writer.

At the very end of *The Fellowship of the Ring*, as Frodo is fleeing from Boromir, he climbs to a tower and is offered a vision of the power of the Dark Lord that is made spectacular by the fact that Frodo is wearing the Ring. Looking north and west he sees all the signs of war: fires, orcs, hordes of warriors and horsemen. Then, looking south, down the river:

> But against Minas Tirith was set another fortress, greater and more strong. Thither, eastward, unwilling his eye was drawn. It passed the ruined bridges of Osgiliath, the grinning gates of Minas Morgul, and the haunted Mountains, and it looked upon Gorgoroth, the valley of terror in the Land of Mordor. Darkness lay there under the Sun. Fire glowed amid the smoke. Mount Doom was burning, and a great reek rising. Then at last his gaze was held: wall upon wall, battlement upon battlement, black, immeasurably strong, mountain of iron, gate of steel, tower of adamant, he saw it: Barad-dur, Fortress of Sauron. All hope left him.

Wearing the Ring gives Frodo superhuman eyesight, able to see the valley on the other side of a mountain range, and to identify the materials used in the making of a fortress in that valley, two hundred miles away. But this power is really Sauron's, not Frodo's, and Tolkien must try to build his rhetoric so that each name, each detail, evokes the horror of that power such that to reach the place where Frodo's gaze is held, Barad-dûr, is to realize that all hope must leave him. Every step Frodo takes after this vision will be solemn, foolish, heroic. To see freshly now is to see reasons for despair—that is the truth of the Myth of Lost Unity operating here—and to go on is to try to move in spite of that despair or those reasons.

Before following Frodo on his journey, we must look at the parts of the last two volumes devoted to the war west of the Anduin, and to see what Tolkien does with the hobbits there. In one place Tolkien succeeds beautifully even though he is not dealing with the Ring, which he usually needs to make his literary language work. In the grand fourth chapter of *The Two Towers*, Merry and Pippin discover the ents in Fangorn. This is much the best detachable episode in the trilogy, the best passage, furthermore, to read aloud to those skeptical of Tolkien to show how he works. One quotation may be enough; Pippin is describing the eyes of the ent Treebeard:

> "One felt as if there was an enormous well behind them,
> filled up with ages of memory and long, slow, steady thinking;
> but their surface was sparkling with the present: like sun
> shimmering on the outer leaves of a vast tree, or on the ripples
> of a very deep lake. I don't know, but it felt as if something that
> grew in the ground—asleep, you might say, or just feeling itself
> as something between root-tip and leaf-tip, between deep earth
> and sky had suddenly waked up, and was considering you with
> the same slow care that it had given to its own inside affairs for
> endless years."

Here is Recovery and escape from ordinary vision because Pippin is seeing the likeness of animal and plant; Treebeard *is* like a tree, but like a lake, too, and a well, and a man. The world is not suddenly alive, but suddenly Pippin sees that it is, and has been for longer than he can guess, and "was considering you with the same slow care that it had given to its own inside affairs for endless years." To be able to write a phrase like that is to be able to show that the aliveness of the world is not just belief for Tolkien. He has taken ancientness from forest, mind from man, color and life from sun and tree, and made an ent; "in such 'fantasy'," as Tolkien has said, "new form is made; Faërie begins; Man becomes a sub-creator."

Unfortunately, much more often in these sections we have something like this, Merry's meeting with Théoden, King of the Mark of Rohan, outside Saruman's castle:

"My people came out of the North long ago," said
Théoden. "But I will not deceive you: we know no tales about
hobbits. All that is said among us is that far away, over many
hills and rivers, live the halfling folk that dwell in holes in sand-
dunes. But there are no legends of their deeds, for it is said that
they do little, and avoid the sight of men, being able to vanish
in a twinkling; and they can change their voices to resemble the
piping of birds. But it seems that more could be said."

"It could indeed, lord," said Merry.

"For one thing," said Théoden, "I had not heard that
they spouted smoke from their mouths."

"That is not surprising," answered Merry; "for it is an art
which we have not practised for more than a few generations.
It was Tobold Hornblower, of Longbottom in the
Southfarthing, who first grew the true pipe-weed in his
gardens, about the year 1070 according to our reckoning. How
old Toby came by the plant . . ."

"You do not know your danger, Théoden," interrupted
Gandalf. "These hobbits will sit on the edge of ruin and discuss
the pleasures of the table, or the small doings of their fathers,
grandfathers, and great-grandfathers, and remoter cousins to
the ninth degree, if you encourage them with undue patience."

It is not Théoden who is unduly patient, but Tolkien, who loves to indulge
himself, with the trite vision of hobbits discussing the pleasures of tobacco
while sitting on the edge of ruin. Merry is not a perceiver here, but a
performer, so there is nothing interesting for Théoden to Recover either.
While this is only irritating, a betrayal of some pact an attentive reader
thought he had made with Tolkien to use his hobbits as Recoverers, it goes
along with something worse, useful only for showing the heroism Tolkien
cannot write well about, the better to show the heroism he can.

The men in Tolkien's world are all cast in rather ancient molds—the
Riders of Rohan are like Dark Age Germanic tribes; the citizens of Gondor
live in a decaying Alexandria or Constantinople. So their heroism is also
ancient: stern, solemn, filled with belief in portents and in absolute loyalty to
tribe and city:

"It is not strong," said Faramir. "I have sent the company
of Ithilien to strengthen it, as I have said."

"Not enough, I deem," said Denethor. "It is there that
the first blow will fall. They will have need of some stout
captain there."

"There and elsewhere in many places," said Faramir, and sighed. "Alas for my brother, whom I too loved!" He rose. "May I have your leave, father?" And then he swayed and leaned upon his father's chair.

"You are weary, I see," said Denethor. "You have ridden fast and far, and under shadows of evil in the air, I am told."

"Let us not speak of that!" said Faramir.

"Then we will not," said Denethor. "Go now and rest as you may. Tomorrow's need will be sterner."

This is so bad that it already seems like an S. J. Perelman parody, and Tolkien is capable of going on for pages like this, without pause for breath or blinking. This Old World of Men is very important to Tolkien in one sense, and he works very hard to have it seem important and impressive. But he simply knows nothing about men, or knows them only through books, and so all he can do is copy down their manners as he has read of them. The fact that he does better with elves and dwarves, and that he does best of all with his own inventions, the hobbits and ents, shows how far he had withdrawn— it is not difficult to see that he intended no irony when he said that a centaur is more "real" than an automobile. The price he had to pay, we can see, is that he is ignorant of men and unaware of his ignorance. So we have, for a while in the second volume and for long stretches at the beginning of the third, false language and false manner that hurts everything; faced with Denethor and Faramir and the others, Pippin and Merry can either clown before them or else talk as they do, which is no choice at all.

To be sure, even the worst sections "fit" into Tolkien's whole conception, though that is nowhere near enough to save them. What keeps them moving is the fullness of Tolkien's intuition about evil, which told him that when Sauron resumed his ancient seat it was not only in Mordor that the shadows lengthened: those lesser than Sauron are smaller, even pettier, in their aims, but no less malicious. Saruman the White Wizard studied Sauron and was corrupted, and so he tried to set himself up as rival conqueror and hunter after the Ring. He enlisted orcs and wolves; he subverted King Théoden of Rohan with a despairing counselor; he had trees cut down wantonly in the forest of Fangorn and thereby aroused the anger of Treebeard the ent; he corrupted some small town toughs far north, in Bree and in The Shire, and had them destroy willfully and meanly. Denethor, steward to the vacant throne of Gondor, also wrestled with Sauron and was deceived, though in his case the deception led not to dreams of conquest but to despair and suicide. The conception does hold up remarkably well. Tolkien needs all Middle Earth to show how evil invades, corrupts, makes small and possessive, because for him evil is not merely Satanic.

Unfortunately, to fulfill this conception Tolkien has to write about people and ways he only knows about rather than knows, and when that happens the writing stiffens and the humorlessness becomes enervating.

But no one has ever rejected *The Lord of the Rings* because of this. In the first place the worst parts come in the third volume and by then the grand expansiveness of the design is so fully felt that the dullness of the writing matters much less than it would had these pages come earlier. In the second place, there are some fine moments here: the end of the battle in Helm's Deep when the ents appear to surround Saruman's forces; the appearance of the Lord of the Nazgûl before the gates of Gondor; the last council, which is Gandalf's finest hour. In the third place, we know while reading these sections that they will eventually give way to the story of Frodo and Sam on the other side of the Anduin in which a much different kind of heroism and a vastly more impressive role for the hobbits can be found. Here all that is promised in the first volume is delivered, and with a rare and wonderful and modern majesty.

The moment we move back across the Anduin to Frodo and Sam, we have landscapes, and for these Tolkien has no background of received tradition on which to draw, and the books he read could not tell him how to proceed. At the end of *The Fellowship of the Ring*, as we have seen, Frodo has his frightening vision of Sauron's power while he is wearing the Ring, and that is enough to show him and us his task. Frodo is of course not big enough to stand up to Sauron; he cannot go on wearing the Ring without sooner or later giving away his presence, so we come down. No one sees the doors of Barad-dûr in a wasteland of crags and gullies called the Emyn Muil:

> The hobbits stood now on the brink of a tall cliff, bare and bleak, its feet wrapped in mist; and behind them rose the broken highlands crowned with drifting cloud. A chill wind blew from the East. Night was gathering over the shapeless lands before them; the sickly green of them was fading to a sullen brown. Far away to the right the Anduin, that had gleamed fitfully in sun-breaks during the day, was now hidden in shadow. But their eyes did not look beyond the River, back to Gondor, to their friends, to the lands of Men. South and east they stared to where, at the edge of the oncoming night, a dark line hung, like distant mountains of motionless smoke.

The route through this world must be made rather than followed, and here Sam Gamgee begins to become more Frodo's equal and less his servant. In the first volume Sam is very much the servant or the slave of the nineteenth century, thinking only of Master Frodo, speaking in a crude slang designed to keep him in his place, tending strictly to domestic and logistical details. But given the trackless wild country through which Frodo and Sam are now moving, all that must give way to an increasing sense of mutual dependency.

Even before this Frodo and Sam are aware that they are being followed, by Sméagol, Gollum, the owner of the Ring before Bilbo. Back at the Council of Elrond, Legolas had said that Sméagol had escaped from the wood-elves who had been his guardians after his capture by Aragorn. Earlier still, after losing the Ring, Sméagol had gone to Mordor, had been broken by Sauron, and had been let go to try to find the Ring again. Now he has tracked the fellowship south, and on the lonely Emyn Muil he meets Sam and Frodo unexpectedly, and they capture him. Sam is all for getting rid of Sméagol, but Frodo remembers something Gandalf had said long ago, back in The Shire:

> "I have not much hope that Gollum can be cured before he dies, but there is a chance of it. And he is bound up with the fate of the Ring. My heart tells me that he has some part to play yet, for good or ill, before the end; and when that comes, the pity of Bilbo [in not killing Gollum] may rule the fate of many—yours not least."

What we have here is more than a prophetic device to frame the story, because Frodo knows more than what Gandalf said. Sam sees Sméagol only as a dangerous nuisance, slithery, cunning, and obviously given to lying. But Frodo himself is feeling the weight of the Ring and can see, as Sam cannot and as Gandalf only could guess, why Gollum is more an object of pity than of scorn or anger. The natural kinship of similar creatures and the common bondage of those who bear the Ring become one:

> "And what would you swear?" asked Frodo.
>
> "To be very very good," said Gollum. Then crawling to Frodo's feet he grovelled before him, whispering hoarsely: a shudder ran over him, as if the words shook his very bones with fear. "Sméagol will swear never, never, to let Him have it. Never! Sméagol will save it. But he must swear on the Precious."
>
> "No! not on it," said Frodo, looking down at him with stern pity. "All you wish is to see it and touch it, if you can, though you know it would drive you mad. Not on it. Swear by it, if you will. For you know where it is. Yes, you know, Sméagol. It is before you."
>
> For a moment it appeared to Sam that his master had grown and Gollum had shrunk: a tall stern shadow, a mighty

lord who hid his brightness in grey cloud, and at his feet a little whining dog. Yet the two were in some way akin and not alien: they could reach one another's minds."

Because outcast, Frodo can create the possibility of society.

One can only hope that Tolkien himself realized that this relationship between Frodo and Sméagol, as seen by Sam, is his masterstroke. In his instinctive wish to save and tame Sméagol rather than destroy him, Frodo creates his heroism. Just as he could see the light of ancient Lothlórien in Aragorn's eyes and so discover and Recover a young but ancient lord, so here he Recovers himself by looking at Gollum at his feet and seeing "himself" there, seeing his own struggle to stay alive against the force of insuperably great power and temptation. He does not know what Sméagol has in mind, and knows he does not know, knows that in Sméagol he sees what he might become very easily if he does not struggle.

Gollum tells Frodo and Sam of his first trip to Mordor:

> "Once, by accident it was, wasn't it, precious? Yes, by accident. But we won't go back, no, no!" Then suddenly his voice and language changed, and he sobbed in his throat, and spoke but not to them. "Leave me alone, *gollum*! You hurt me. O my poor hands, *gollum*! I, we, I don't want to come back. I can't find it. I am tired. I, we can't find it, *gollum*, *gollum*, no, nowhere. They're always awake. Dwarves, Men, and Elves, terrible Elves with bright eyes. I can't find it. Ach!"

Sméagol is the expert on the journey because he also is the historian, the one who knows where they are going because he has been there. In this scene Frodo can see the past just as he could in the one with Aragorn in Lothlórien. Needing all that Sméagol can tell them, even though he can only guess when he is being told the truth, Frodo knows he must let Gollum guide them.

They travel by night and sleep by day. They move out of the gullies of the Emyn Muil and into the Dead Marshes, where lights like candles flicker in stagnant pools. Earlier Strider and Gandalf and Galadriel had told Frodo where he was by saying what had happened there; here Sméagol brings the Dead Marshes to "life":

> "Yes. yes," said Gollum. "All dead, all rotten. Elves and Men and Orcs. The Dead Marshes. There was a great battle long ago, yes, so they told him when Sméagol was young, when I was young before the Precious came. It was a great battle. Tall Men with long swords, and terrible Elves, and Orcses

shrieking. They fought on the plain for days and months at the Black Gates. But the Marshes have grown since then, swallowed up the graves; always creeping, creeping."

We understand the landscape by understanding history, and it is as though we are living through a microcosmic history of the Western world, so that long after the great battles, the hobbits come wandering in the Dead Marshes with an untrustworthy guide.

Then a Nazgûl looms up, "a black shadow loosed from Mordor; a vast shape winged and ominous . . . sweeping the fen-reek with its ghastly wings." When it leaves "Frodo and Sam got up, rubbing their eyes, like children wakened from an evil dream to find the familiar night still over the world." Not knowing which is worse, the "unreal" Ringwraith or the "real" Dead Marshes, they cower and hope uncertainly during the day, groping their way at night. Then, one dawn, "Frodo looked round in horror":

> Dreadful as the Dead Marshes had been, and the arid moors of No-men's Land, more loathsome far was the country that the crawling day now slowly unveiled to his shrinking eyes. Even to the Mere of Dead Faces some haggard phantom of green spring would come; but here neither spring nor summer would ever come again. Here nothing lived, not even the leprous growths that feed on rottenness. The gasping pools were choked with ash and crawling muds, sickly white and grey, as if the mountains had vomited the filth of their entrails upon the lands about. High mounds of crushed and powdered rock, great cones of earth fire-blasted and poison-stained, stood like an obscene graveyard in endless rows, slowly revealed in the reluctant light.

Children, lost on the way to the mountains of their doom, led by a wretched sniveling wight—in this bleakest of landscapes, now recognizably modern, every act is heroic. The old terms for the struggle of good against evil—courage, loyalty, honor, magnificence, fortitude—are mostly irrelevant now. We notice another of those brilliant repetitions of a verb that makes a metaphor out of two nouns: the day and the mud both "crawl," so the light is indeed "reluctant." This is the industrial slag of midlands England, and No Man's Land in France in 1916, and so we come closer and closer to the modern evil that is Sauron:

> *One Ring to rule them all, One Ring to find them,*
> *One Ring to bring them all and in the darkness bind them*

The ordering of such a deathly landscape is Sauron's triumph, and we may well remember that the trilogy is called *The Lord of the Rings*. It is his book, and Frodo can only become more bound to the Ring the closer he comes to Sauron. In the Marshes, on these foul plains before the Black Gate, then down the dark road to Minas Morgul, up the stairs into the mountains to Cirith Ungol—all that way we have no fight against evil but the effort to stay alive and the consequences of giving in to death.

So, though Tolkien may have been enabled to return to this vision of modern life by withdrawing, Frodo cannot hold back at all. Inevitably he becomes less able to do more than merely walk, and Sam must assume command. Frodo's last great effort comes after the stairs have been climbed and the hobbits discover that Sméagol has reached his destination, and kept his promise not to deliver the Ring into Sauron's hands. Instead, he has taken them to Shelob, a giant spiderlike creature who lives in the caves near the top of the mountains:

> There agelong she had dwelt, an evil thing in spider-form, even such as once of old had lived in the Land of the Elves in the West that is now under the Sea, such as Beren fought in the Mountains of Terror in Doriath, and so came to Lúthien upon the green sward amid the hemlocks in the moonlight long ago. How Shelob came there, flying from ruin, no tale tells, for out of the Dark Years few tales have come.

The lore pours out wantonly, and we sense in the story of Beren a nostalgic glance on Tolkien's part back to a world he would much rather have lived in than the one he in fact did, but his sense of the present is so strong that the glance is recognizably and almost consciously placed as being nostalgic, and the lore that describes Shelob herself is anything but that:

> Already, years before, Gollum had beheld her, Sméagol who pried into all dark holes, and in past days he had bowed and worshipped her, and the darkness of her evil will walked through all the ways of his weariness beside him, cutting him off from light and from regret. And he had promised to bring her food. But her lust was not his lust. Little she knew of or cared for towers, or rings, or anything devised by mind or hand, who only desired death for all others, mind and body, and for herself a glut of life, alone, swollen till the mountains could no longer hold her up and the darkness could not contain her.

For a moment Sauron himself becomes kin to the hobbits, caring for towers and rings, things devised by mind and hand as he does, and, by comparison with Shelob, he is lofty in his aims and lusts.

We then learn why Gollum has brought the hobbits here: "It may well be, O yes, it may well be that when She throws away the bones and the empty garments, we shall find it, we shall get it, the Precious." Also, and inevitably, Frodo is becoming like Gollum because of the burden of the Ring, himself almost cut off from the light and from regret in all the ways of *his* weariness. But it is still "almost": he has light, in a vial given him by Galadriel, and he has a sword given him by Bilbo, so he fights and wounds Shelob. But he falls too, and Sam is left in a quandary. First he decides to go on alone with the Ring, then he follows a group of orcs who have dragged Frodo's body away, and finally, after resisting the temptation to put on the Ring and become a hero, he climbs into a large chamber where an orc stands with a whip over something lying on the floor. Sam rushes at the orc and wins the fight only because the orc accidentally falls through an open trapdoor. He then turns and finds that it is Frodo on the floor, alive, but wounded and weak, unable to move any farther with his burden without help. So Sam must guide them now as Sméagol had done earlier, and Frodo's greatness lies in part in his ability to know this, and to seek and gain the help and community of others because he cannot move alone. But the price he is paying is awful, as we see when he discovers that Sam now has the Ring, and he almost falls to pieces, Gollum-like:

> "Give it to me" he cried, standing up, holding out a trembling hand. "Give it me at once! You can't have it!"
>
> "All right, Mr. Frodo," said Sam, rather startled. "Here it is!" Slowly he drew the Ring out and passed the chain over his head. "But you're in the land of Mordor now, sir; and when you get out, you'll see the Fiery Mountain and all. You'll find the Ring very dangerous now, and very hard to bear. If it's too hard a job, I could share it with you, maybe?"

Sam senses how terrible the burden is going to be for Frodo and also, he wants the Ring, if only in some small way, for himself. But Frodo can only see in Sam's want a reflection of his own much greater want, cut off as he is from light and from regret, bound and binding:

> "No, no!" cried Frodo, snatching the Ring and chain from Sam's hands. "No you won't, you thief!" He panted, staring at Sam with eyes wide with fear and enmity.

For that moment Frodo is himself Sméagol, but then:

> A mist seemed to clear from his eyes, and he passed a hand over
> his aching brow. The hideous vision had seemed so real to him,
> half bemused as he was still with wound and fear. Sam had
> changed before his very eyes into an orc again, leering and
> pawing at his treasure, a foul little creature with greedy eyes
> and slobbering mouth. But now the vision had passed. There
> was Sam kneeling before him, his face wrung with pain, as if he
> had been stabbed in the heart.

Tolkien cannot say that Frodo is heroic because for him the passing of the
awful vision is simply and implicitly part of Frodo's goodness, his aliveness;
no act of will is involved. But we know that modern heroism need not and
probably even cannot carry with it any strong conscious sense of willed
achievement or triumph; for Frodo not to "triumph" over Sam is his
heroism. He is Frodo still.

The hideous moment passed, Sam helps Frodo on with an orc uniform
and they escape the tower to the valley of the Morgai. Gandalf has lured
Sauron's army out beyond the mountains by pretending that the combined
forces of Rohan and Gondor and elsewhere can actually challenge the armies
of the Dark Lord, and he has done this knowing that the only possible help
he could provide Frodo, assuming that Frodo is still alive, is in that lure.
Frodo and Sam watch Sauron's armies march past them and out to the Black
Gate, so that the road to Barad-dur is almost deserted, but Frodo is
nonetheless almost helpless. Sam has to carry him part way up Mount Doom,
the end of the journey, but when they reach the brink of the chasm where the
Ring was forged, Sam hears Frodo, and in a voice "clearer and more
powerful than Sam had ever heard him use":

> "I have come," he said. "But I do not choose now to do what
> I came to do. I will not do this deed. The Ring is mine!" And
> suddenly, as he set it on his finger, he vanished from Sam's sight.

If the story were Frodo's to shape to his will, all would be lost, his heroism at
last unavailing, his binding to the Dark Lord complete. But it is not his.
Suddenly Sméagol is there, knocking Sam down and pursuing the vanished
Frodo. Sauron too leaps in response:

> From all his policies and webs of fear and treachery, from
> all his stratagems and wars his mind shook free; and
> throughout his realm a tremor ran, his slaves quailed, and his

armies halted, and his captains suddenly steerless, bereft of will, wavered and despaired. . . . At his summons, wheeling with a rending cry, in a last desperate race there flew, faster than the winds, the Nazgûl, the Ringwraiths, and with a storm of wings they hurtled southwards to Mount Doom.

But too late, Gollum is there first, struggling with the invisible Frodo. Sauron once had lost the Ring when Isildur cut it from his hand, and so now Frodo, Lord of the Rings for a moment, is attacked:

Suddenly Sam saw Gollum's long hands draw upwards to his mouth; his white fangs gleamed, and then snapped as they bit. Frodo gave a cry, and there he was, fallen upon his knees at the chasm's edge.

Gollum shouts that the prize is his, "And with that, even as his eyes were lifted up to gloat on his prize, he stepped too far, toppled, wavered for a moment on the brink, and then with a shriek he fell." As the Ring falls to its doom the mountain shakes; outside

Towers fell and mountains slid; walls crumbled and melted, crashing down; vast spires of smoke and spouting steams went billowing up, up, until they toppled like an overwhelming wave, and its wild crest curled and came foaming down upon the land.

This is fairy tale, and the Ring must destroy Sauron's world apocalyptically. But it is Frodo and Sméagol—neither of whom is grand, neither of whom at that last moment sought the Ring's destruction—who are responsible. Wars have always been secondary in this struggle, and at the end even Frodo's modern heroism, which is of primary importance, is unavailing:

"Well, this is the end, Sam Gamgee," said a voice by his side. And there was Frodo, pale and worn, and yet himself again; and in his eyes there was peace now, neither strain of will, nor madness, nor any fear. His burden was taken away.

The phrasing of that last sentence is precise, as Frodo makes clear right away. His burden was taken from him by the only one whose need to make the Ring his own was at that moment greater than Frodo's own. Peaceful though he is now, Frodo is bound still, and he must seek solace and compassion for his bound companion Sméagol.

In the end they are rescued and returned, first to Gondor where Aragorn is crowned, then to The Shire, where the hobbits discover to their surprise and outrage that Saruman's cronies have been wanton, tearing down trees, setting up petty governments. The trouble here can be righted, however. Saruman is discovered, conquered, exiled, and killed, and afterward trees can be planted again, Sam can marry Rosie Cotton, and even eventually become Mayor. But for Frodo all is unreal; he could not fight much against Saruman, his wounds cannot heal, his bondage cannot be broken, he cannot really settle down in The Shire, though he tries. Merry and Pippin are now lore-masters in The Shire, with their tales of Rohan and Gondor and battles. Frodo, however, "dropped quietly out of all the doings of the Shire, and Sam was pained to notice how little honour he had in his own country." In an earlier age, we may remember, heroic deeds were rewarded with instant glory and renown. The Faerie Queene could know of and honor the deeds of any of her knights almost the moment they happened. In Shakespearean tragedy the hero is never properly understood by those around him, but Hamlet is given a soldier's burial and Lear's death is greeted, as Empson says, "with a sort of hushed envy." But for Frodo none of that is possible: "It is gone for ever," he says, half in a dream, "and now all is dark and empty." So he leaves The Shire and goes westward to the Grey Havens where, with Gandalf and the faded elves, he sets out to sea. He knows that this "defeat" is natural, that he was part of an age that is passing, that he was one of the instruments of its passing indeed, and a securer of the world's living. There is bang, then, in the destruction of Mordor, but whimper too in Frodo's discovery that his wounds cannot heal on Middle Earth.

So Frodo is finally of his time, just as Tolkien is of his, and both realize (Frodo perhaps better than Tolkien about this) that one can only live in the time in which he was born. Tolkien could write of Gandalf and elves and of ancient men, but because they were not of his time he could write of them only what he had read in books, and the resultant literariness never leaves them. Likewise he writes so wonderfully about Frodo because, by comparison with the others, Frodo is a modern, his landscape, his challenge, and his heroism all distinctively belonging to no earlier century.

"That virtue and intelligence are alike lonely," writes Empson at the end of *Pastoral*, "and that good manners are therefore important though an absurd confession of human limitations, do not depend on a local class system; they would be recognised in a degree by any tolerable society." Temperamentally there is little resemblance between Empson and Tolkien, for Empson is subtle and cheerful and pagan and Tolkien none of these. But Empson's sentence does as well in describing Tolkien's and Frodo's greatness as anything Tolkien himself might have tried to say in summary. When we look at *The Lord of the Rings* in retrospect, we see that Sauron cannot openly affect Frodo at all; valor and physical strength and the very idea of battles are not germane here. Sauron can bind Frodo only as Frodo binds himself and seeks to bind others, his virtue and his intelligence alike lonely, cut off from lore and aid. The landscape through which Frodo must move is Sauron's most powerful weapon, a valley of the shadow of death, and we know there are ways to see the book as being Christian and Frodo as a pilgrim. But the landscape is really much closer, as we have said, to the wasteland, the valley of ashes, and the nightmare cities of Rupert Birkin and Henry Adams than it is to the arbitrary and unclear landscapes of Spenser or Bunyan. Where Tolkien differs most from other modern writers is not in what he sees but in what he understands must be done.

If Frodo's virtue and intelligence must be lonely, then one way of describing his heroism is to reaffirm his "good manners," though that is not the most obvious way of saying it. In different ways both Sam Gamgee and Sméagol are better equipped than is Frodo to carry the Ring to Mordor. But they are also less virtuous, less intelligent, less courteous; they cannot sympathize or trust each other and they cannot understand Frodo's sympathy and trust for them both. Sam serves Frodo, Sméagol serves the Ring, and only Frodo can serve the heroic idea of the Ring's destruction. Yet though neither Sam nor Sméagol is of Frodo's stature, he is lost without them, and he knows it. His good manners toward both is an absurd confession of limitations of any so lonely, yet in his love for Sam and compassion for Sméagol he finds himself. As long as Frodo is thus openly dependent, the urge to possessiveness can be quelled by his good manners and his recognition of the blessed and cursed otherness of his servant and his wretched guide.

In a moment of respite on the stairs of Cirith Ungol, just before Sméagol takes them to Shelob, Frodo and Sam talk about the songs that will be sung of them after all this is over. Sam does most of the talking, but Frodo makes the key points: (1) "You may know, or guess, what kind of a tale it is, happy-ending or sad-ending, but the people in it don't know. And you don't want them to." (2) "[The great tales] never end as tales. . . . But the people in them come, and go when their part's ended." (3) "Why, Sam . . . to hear you somehow makes me as merry as if the story was already written. But you've left out one of the chief characters: Samwise the stouthearted. . . . 'And Frodo wouldn't have got far without Sam, would he. . . . '" (4) "It's no good worrying about him [Sméagol] now. . . . We couldn't have got so far, not even within sight of the pass, without him, and so we'll have to put up with his ways. If he's false, he's false."

We are in a story, but we have as yet no storyteller, only ourselves—such is Frodo's meaning and it is rather too much for Sam. But Sam does recognize the grim and yet almost sublime equipoise of Frodo's weary generosity—I cannot come upon this pending passage without feeling simply grateful to Frodo for being what he is here—and so, too, for a moment, does Sméagol. Right after this conversation Frodo and Sam fall asleep and Sméagol discovers them thus, peaceful in each other's arms:

> A strange expression passed over his lean hungry face. The gleam faded from his eyes, and they went dim and grey, old and tired. A spasm of pain seemed to twist him, and he turned away, peering back up towards the pass, shaking his head, as if engaged in some interior debate. Then he came back, and slowly putting out a trembling hand, very cautiously he touched Frodo's knee—but almost the touch was a caress. For a fleeting moment, could one of the sleepers have seen him, they would have thought that they beheld an old weary hobbit, shrunken by the years that had carried him far beyond his time, beyond friends and kin, and the fields and streams of youth, an old starved pitiable thing.

This is Sméagol's finest moment, and so it must be Frodo's and Tolkien's finest moment too. Beyond friends and kin, old, tired, Sméagol loves the specialness that is Frodo's care of him. This love is almost without its like in our modern literature, because it is not filial or sexual but the tentative, unbelieving response to a caring so unlikely it seems heroic even to Gollum. It suggests the story might go differently, but not just Frodo and Sméagol are bound here, possessive, but Sam as well. He wakes before Frodo and automatically accuses Sméagol of being a sneak. By the time Frodo wakes Gollum is back to his old whining and sniveling self, ready once again to lead the hobbits to Shelob.

Frodo's uniqueness and greatness lie in his way of being returned to himself as he sees a light shine in others; no one else in the trilogy, really, can do this more than fitfully. He faces the strongest of temptations to give in and to make the world only what he says it is, but of all the characters he shows fewest signs of having yielded to that temptation. He turns out into the world and so finds a means of self-knowledge, and in his scarred and beautiful relation with Sméagol he finds himself and lives by the light of the self he finds. He is saved from the worst ravages of the Ring because of his lovely courtesy that lets others be themselves and unbound, and therein finds a way to be heroic. This heroism may not be what *The Lord of the Rings* is all about, and almost certainly it is not all that it is good for, in Tolkien's scheme or anyone else's, but it is the cornerstone of its greatness. Over and over we are told of the prices that must be paid when one is called upon to pay them, and over and over Gandalf, Aragorn, Merry, Pippin, Faramir, and others pay such prices when they are demanded. But these are ancient heroisms, ancient prices and payments, and Frodo's heroism is not, and as all the "great deeds" are chronicled, we respond to what is most like ourselves because Tolkien does too. We see, without in the least needing to make that seeing into a formulation, what this version of modern heroism is and can be: lonely, lost, frightened, loving, willing, and compassionate—to recognize the otherness of others while reaching out to assert our common livingness.

Tolkien published *The Lord of the Rings* in the mid-fifties, when he was nearing retirement. Shortly thereafter word began to filter down from people who may or may not have actually talked to Tolkien, that he was at work on something called *The Silmarillion*, which was also about Middle Earth. That Tolkien has occupied this place of his with far more than ever got into the tale of the Rings is clear enough from the hundred pages of appendixes that recount tales and give genealogies of hobbits, dwarves, elves, and men that were published at the end of the third volume of the trilogy. Presumably *The Silmarillion*, which may be prose or poetry or written in Elvish, concerns itself with some of this material. In the meantime, perhaps in response to public cry for "more Tolkien," he allowed to be published *The Adventures of Tom Bombadil*, an exceedingly bad collection of hobbit poems; it barely makes a good Christmas gift for members of the Tolkien cult. Nor should one find hope in the promised *Silmarillion*. At this writing Tolkien is still alive and said to be at work, but he is also in his late seventies and there is no earthly reason why he should not be working in ways that amuse him privately and that maintain his withdrawal from all he finds abhorrent in contemporary life. Empson may speak of once again facing unresolved conflicts when one is "seriously old," but Tolkien's passage always was far different from Empson's. The conflicts of Empson's youth he faced, heroically, with his pastoral triumph over them. Then, as he has said, the conflicts were reduced or transformed into practical questions, and, as we have seen, into doctrinal answers. Tolkien, however, had to run from his conflicts, to find in his imagined Middle Earth Recovery not just things "as they were meant to be seen" but recovery from the oppressive wounds of the war, and it was only in fairy tale, in myth, that he could face and resolve the conflicts at all. It took years to accomplish this, Tolkien was writing about the pains and terrors of his twenties when he was in his fifties, and that in itself is miracle enough that one should not hope or ask that he should ever try again. Tolkien has never said anything to lead one to believe that he recognizes that what is greatest and most poignant in his imagination is its modernity, and anyone who tried to convince him of this would be both foolish and rude. Anyone who has read the denigrators of *The Lord of the Rings* knows how silly they can be when they try to make Tolkien out to be dangerously old-fashioned. The latest to come to my attention is by Catherine Stimpson in the Columbia Essays on Modern Writers series, and it makes great point of the fact that the women in Tolkien are not much, that Shelob herself is a terrifying Giant Mother, that symbolism of white and black, light and dark, is pernicious in our day and age. That all this is true enough in its way is only another way of saying that it is irrelevant, that except for his two lectures everything Tolkien wrote outside the trilogy is not very good, that *The Silmarillion* is not a work one can hope much for if one is not a cultist—that, in other words, *The Lord of the Rings* is something of a miracle.

One can only guess, but it does seem that Tolkien's having had to take over thirty years before he could write his heroic book about war hurt its chances of being read properly. Had he been able to write *The Lord of the Rings* at the same age that Lawrence and Empson were when they wrote their greatest books, the year would have been about 1922, and the way it rises to its greatest heights in its response to the circumstances of the modern world and the Great War should have been clear to many. By the fifties the modern age had passed and the war that did most to define it had been forgotten or else never known by those who read and adored Tolkien, and so *The Lord of the Rings* became a book fearfully abused. It afforded a withdrawal that was far less understandable or necessary than Tolkien's own in the years after 1918; it afforded ways of being chic and adolescently melancholy, too, and what it afforded beyond that was misunderstood or ignored.

For such a failure, however, we should not blame only the members of the Tolkien cult. This much is true about the heroism of our century, and it is probably truer of our century than of some earlier ones: it is rare, and it is not easy to recognize. A great deal of this book has concerned itself in one way or another with the reasons why this should be so, and if readers of Tolkien in the fifties and sixties could not see how he and Frodo are modern heroes, let us add right away that no one seems to know, as yet, what postmodern or contemporary heroism is. I can only hope here that something like recognition for Tolkien's heroism, and for Lawrence's and Empson's as well, can at least show that we had heroes as recently as a generation ago and that there is no necessary reason why we will never have any again.

History is always creating the conditions of chaos, and for most people, undoubtedly, some grim or comic adaptation to those conditions is all that is possible or necessary. But it is in our nature to seek to reply to history as well as to acknowledge it, and if it is still true that the hero resembles the fool because he does what most of us would never do, we can and should understand that fact. Lawrence and Empson and Tolkien are not likely heroes, but then few ever are. In any age there is much to admire that is not heroic at all, but we deny much that has been achieved and much that may still be possible if we once imagine there can be no more heroes. Most intelligent and sensitive people at any time despair of the present and the future, and with good reason, too. But it is not the only way.

DANIEL GROTTA-KURSKA

The Author (1953–1965)

After reading *The Lord of the Rings* manuscript in its entirety for the first
time, Raynor Unwin had no doubt in his mind that it was a work of absolute
genius. He also had no doubt that Allen & Unwin would publish the book,
and furthermore, no doubt that the firm would probably lose £1,000 ($2,800)
on it. As William Cater aptly pointed out in a London *Sunday Times*
magazine article on Tolkien, "What is remarkable is that *The Lord of the
Rings*, on which Tolkien's fame depends, had all the earmarks of a publishing
disaster. A book for the adult market, at an adult price, it continued the story
of *The Hobbit*, which was a children's book; it ran to three volumes, longer
than *War and Peace*; it contained stretches of verse, five learned appendices
[not all in the original edition, however], and samples of imaginary languages
in imaginary alphabets; but only the most slender 'romantic interest.' It was
concerned with good and evil, honor, endurance and heroism, in an
imaginary age of our world, and was described by its author as 'largely an
essay in linguistic aesthetics.'"

Raynor Unwin did not have the authority to commit the firm to what
seemed to be an inevitable financial loss; the only person who could make
such a decision was his father, Sir Stanley Unwin, and he was away on
business in Japan and the Far East. Raynor Unwin sent a cablegram to his
father asking authority to publish the book, stating that in his opinion, it was

From *J. R. R. Tolkien: Architect of Middle Earth*. A Biography by Daniel Grotta-Kurska, edited by
Frank Wilson. © 1976 by Running Press.

a work of genius, but that it would probably cost the firm £1,000 in losses. Sir Stanley cabled back to his son: IF YOU THINK IT A WORK OF GENIUS THEN YOU MAY LOSE £1,000.

Many publishing firms exercise to some degree a policy of patronage for well-written or important works that would bring to the firm prestige, if not profits. Most of the poetry printed in the United States by major publishing houses does not even pay its own way, let alone make a profit; but it continues to be published because it is, in part, "subsidized" by best-sellers and money-making works of lesser genius issued by the same houses. Many publishing houses have an unofficial annual "allotment" of books that they publish strictly on merit and not on profit potential. To Allen & Unwin, Tolkien's book fit into this category, and no one ever expected it to make enough money just to break even. By American standards, the loss of £1,000, or $2,800, seems negligible, even for the early 50's. After all, a large publishing house like Doubleday or Random House may issue an average of a book a day and deal with annual budgets in the tens of millions. But English publishers, for the most part, do not enjoy the mass circulation, or the advantageous financial arrangements, of their American counterparts; in 1953, their total budgets were measured in thousands of pounds, not millions of dollars. This difference meant that a "subsidy" of £1,000 was, relatively speaking, a large amount and therefore a major commitment, in return for which Allen & Unwin hoped to gain favorable reviews, good will, perhaps a literary prize, a well-rounded seasonal list, and other less tangible benefits. Playing patron to works of art was not pure altruism on Sir Stanley Unwin's part; he expected, and usually got, something back for his money.

Once the decision to go ahead was made, Raynor Unwin began applying his skills as a publisher to help minimize the projected loss. The text could not be edited or cut down. (Apparently, very little was ever done by Allen & Unwin to change Tolkien's own version, possibly on the premise that one should not tamper with great literature, but more likely out of the realization that such a task would require an editor with the skills of a philologist and a mythologer.) So the book's length made necessary a substantial investment in paper, ink, typesetting, and binding. Raynor Unwin wanted to minimize the risk that a single large volume would not sell out even a modest first printing and would be remaindered; so he decided to split Tolkien's single large work into *three* small books; *The Fellowship of the Ring*, *The Two Towers*, and *The Return of the King*. In addition, publication dates of the three books would be staggered over a three-year period so as not to incur so large a loss at one time. Furthermore, working on the usually accurate premise that each subsequent volume would have diminished sales, Raynor Unwin scheduled a progressively smaller printing run for each book.

The Fellowship of the Ring was to be issued in an edition of 3,500 in 1954; *The Two Towers* in an edition of 3,250 in 1955, and *The Return of the King* in an edition of only 3,000 the following year.

Actually, the numbers above the 3,000 mark in English publishing reflect an average, and not a small-sized edition. The reason the initial runs were to be high relative to the projected modest sales was that Tolkien's American publisher, Houghton Mifflin, had agreed to issue the trilogy in the United States, but did not wish to risk investing money in printing their own edition. Instead, they followed a practice common to publishers on both sides of the Atlantic, importing unbound sheets (sections of a book) already printed abroad and binding them under their own imprint. This saved Houghton Mifflin the cost of book design, typesetting, and printing. In doing this, they were making a wise business move, but it was to cost everyone involved dearly a decade later.

Initially, Tolkien opposed issuing *The Lord of the Rings* in three parts. He argued that it was a single, unified work, and should be published as such. But Allen & Unwin reminded Tolkien of the hard economic realities of the publishing industry, that it was their money being risked, and that they ought to have a measure of control over the form the book was to take. Tolkien acquiesced to their decision. (The nearest to a complaint Tolkien voiced was to an American interviewer. "But of course it's not a trilogy. That was just a publisher's device.") So his book was published in its entirety and Allen & Unwin even encouraged him to prepare an appendix to and an index for the work.

Preparing *The Lord of the Rings* for publication was not an easy task: the typesetting required extra keys for accents, Elvish script, etc. Mistakes were unusually easy to make, given the large number of proper names and references, and both copyeditors and proofreaders had to be especially meticulous in their work. Then there was the question of the dust jacket, its design, and the illustration and the blurbs thereon. Allen & Unwin felt it inappropriate to write a self-congratulating blurb extolling the artistry of the work or the brilliance of the writing, and thought it inadvisable as well to write a glowing biography of the author. Yet it was almost impossible to write so short a synopsis of the story. Ultimately, Allen & Unwin commissioned three prominent English literary figures, C. S. Lewis, Richard Hughes, and Naomi Mitchison, each to write his own perspective on the work, with one individual's review appearing on one of the three books. This unusual procedure was an excellent way of introducing *The Lord of the Rings* to the most knowledgeable section of the reading public, and of insuring it was reviewed in the major English dailies. It also suggested with a certain stamp of authority that the work was *not* a mere fairy-story, but a mature work reflecting great imagination and brilliant writing.

Allen & Unwin released the first volume, *The Fellowship of the Ring*, with some fanfare in 1954. It received a few passing notices in the press, but most reviewers seemed to hold back until the complete work was issued. One review was by Lewis himself; it appeared in *Time and Tide*. Lewis wrote "Here are beauties which pierce like swords or burn like cold iron; here is a book that will break your heart . . . good beyond hope." The *Guardian* said that Tolkien was a "born story-teller," and the *New Statesman & Nation* (now the *New Statesman*) thought, "It is a story magnificently told, with every kind of color, movement, and greatness."

At first, *The Fellowship of the Ring* had steady but unexciting sales. But Allen & Unwin, as well as Houghton Mifflin, were gratified that the book sold better than expected and that the entire first printing would probably be sold. Meanwhile, some academics in England and America discovered the work and spread their interest and enthusiasm to their colleagues. An example of this underground excitement over the book is revealed in a eulogy to Tolkien published four days after his death by the Oxford *Mail*; the eulogy was written by an Oxford don who had been a research student when *The Fellowship of the Ring* had been first published. "Towards the end of my last long vacation when a past graduate student at Oxford," wrote Dr. John Grassi, "another book about another imaginary land written by another Oxford scholar had been published. By happy accident I happened to buy the book almost on the day of publication. The discovery of that book and the world to which it gave entrance was as profoundly exciting and as joyous an experience as had been the discovery of the world of Alice. The book, of course, was *The Fellowship of the Ring*, the first volume of the trilogy which has made the name of J. R. R. Tolkien as immediately recognizable throughout the world as that of Lewis Carroll.

"I read that first volume three times before the publication some months later of the second volume of the trilogy and was, indeed, lucky to be able to do so for the book was scarcely ever in my own possession. It passed from hand to hand among my fellow postgraduate students and for the whole of that academic year our conversation was as much about Middle-earth as about our maturing theses and job prospects.

"For there was a price to be paid for the privilege of being the first generation of Tolkienians which millions who have joined our ranks since can scarcely appreciate. That price was the protracted and intolerable suspense in which we lived in the period before the publication of the second and third volumes, not knowing what the final outcome was to be.

"I never knew him," concluded Dr. Grassi, "but then I never knew Lewis Carroll."

Reports of similar experiences came from other English and American campuses, mostly among graduate students and staff who were most likely and best able to recognize and appreciate the scholarship that went into the work. Those libraries that had been fortunate enough to possess copies of the books found them permanently disappearing off the shelves, and when they were put on reserve shelves, long waiting lists developed. Both Allen & Unwin and Houghton Mifflin sold out the first printing many months before they expected.

But the first inkling Allen & Unwin had that *The Lord of the Rings* was likely to turn a profit occurred when "real" people began writing to them not only to ask when, but to demand that they speed up publication of the remaining volumes. In the publishing industry, it is highly unusual for any book to elicit so popular a response; normally such requests are the result of a calculated campaign by friends of the author. Students, scholars, professional people, teachers, and many others wrote to Allen & Unwin in England and to Houghton Mifflin in America to express their enthusiasm. At that point, Tolkien's publisher realized for the first time that the book had a universal appeal, and not just a narrow following among academics. The trickle of letters became a steady stream, whereupon Sir Stanley Unwin decided to accelerate the publication schedule of the two remaining books. Instead of dropping from 3,500 to 3,250 printed copies for *The Two Towers* and 3,000 for *The Return of the King*, Sir Stanley inverted the "pyramid" policy and increased the number of printed copies. He then concluded that two years was too long a time to wait for the release of the complete work, and published *The Two Towers* six months, and not a year, after *The Fellowship of the Ring*. *The Two Towers* appeared in early 1955, and Tolkien was pressed to complete his expanded appendices and index as soon as possible for early release of *The Return of the King*. Instead of having two years in which to complete work on the addenda, Tolkien suddenly had only six months. The amount of time was woefully insufficient for the monumental task of indexing and completing the appendix, especially since Tolkien still had his professorial responsibilities and had been, for the most part, working alone on the book. When Allen & Unwin released the last volume in the autumn of 1955, they had to announce in a publisher's note that they "Regret that it has not been possible to include as an appendix to this edition the index of names announced in the Preface of *The Fellowship of the Ring*."

Once the entire work was published, many important magazines and newspapers in both England and America assigned it for review. In the main, the reviews were enthusiastically favorable, praising the Professor's originality, imaginative style, epic narration, and sensitive descriptions of nature. One critic said that *The Lord of the Rings* was an onomasthologist's [someone who studies the origin and history of proper names] delight," and another thought it "super science fiction." Others compared it to Mallory and Ariosto, and a couple went so far as to say that Tolkien was superior to them. In America, the New York *Herald Tribune* reviewer called it "an extraordinary, a distinguished piece of work." The Boston *Herald Traveler* described it as "one of the best wonder-tales ever written—and one of the best-written," and W. A. Auden wrote in the *New York Times* that Tolkien "succeeded more completely than any previous writer in this genre in using the traditional properties of the Quest, the heroic journey, the Numinous Object. . . . satisfying our sense of historical and social reality." Auden concluded that Tolkien "has succeeded where Milton failed." Michael Straight wrote in the *New Republic* that "Tolkien's trilogy is fantasy, but it stems of course from Tolkien's own experiences and beliefs. There are scenes of devastation that recall his memories of the Western Front where he fought in the First World War. The description of a snowstorm in a high pass is drawn from a mountain-climbing trip in Switzerland. And through the descriptions of life in Hobbiton and Bywater runs his own bemused love of the English and his scorn for the ugliness of the industrial surroundings in which they live. But Tolkien shuns satire as frivolous and allegory as tendentious. His preparation is immersion in Welsh, Norse, Gaelic, Scandinavian and German folklore. . . . There are very few works of genius in recent literature. This is one."

But the longest and most important review given to *The Lord of the Rings* was decidedly negative. Edmund Wilson, America's protean literary critic, wrote a review titled "Oo, Those Awful Orcs!" in the April 14, 1956 issue of *The Nation* in which he said that *The Lord of the Rings* "is essentially a children's book, which has somehow gotten out of hand. . . . The Author has indulged himself in developing the fantasy for its own sake." After berating Tolkien for his pretentious introduction, Wilson continued that the "prose and verse are on the same level of professional amateurishness. . . . What we get is a simple confrontation—in more or less the traditional terms of British melodrama—of the Forces of Evil with the Forces of Good, the remote and alien villain with the plucky little home-grown hero. . . . Dr. Tolkien has little skill at narrative and no instinct for literary form. The characters talk a story-book language that might have come out of Howard Pyle, and as personalities they do not impose themselves. At the end of this long romance, I still had no conception of the wizard Gandalph [sic], who is a cardinal figure, and had never been able to visualize him at all. For the most part such characterizations as Dr. Tolkien is able to contrive are perfectly stereotyped: Frodo the good little Englishman. Samwise, his doglike servant, who talks lower-class and respectful, and never deserts his master. These characters who are no characters are involved in interminable adventures the poverty of invention displayed in which is, it seems to me, almost pathetic. . . . An impotence of imagination seems to me to sap the whole story. The wars are never dynamic; the ordeals give no sense of strain; the fair ladies would not stir a heartbeat; the horrors would not hurt a fly." Wilson continued in such a vein right to the end of the review, finding no particular merit whatever in the work.

Tolkien was unexpectedly sensitive to the negative reviews. He was depressed that in Great Britain none of the Catholic publications reviewed it favorably (many declined to review it at all), and that the country's most important Catholic journal, *The Tablet*, gave it a lukewarm reception. (He was later mollified when two Catholic publications in the United States and New Zealand gave glowing reviews.) When an interviewer once suggested that *The Lord of the Rings* seemed to have been written for boys rather than for girls, Tolkien took issue and explained that it was necessarily masculine because of the nature of the subject matter. "These are wars and a terrible expedition to the North Pole, so to speak. Surely there is no lack of interest, is there? I know that one interviewer explained it: It is written by a man who has never reached puberty and knows nothing about women but as a schoolboy, and all the good characters come home like happy boys, safe from the war. I thought it was very rude—so far as I know, the man is childless— writing about a man surrounded by children, wife, daughter, granddaughter. Still, that's equally untrue, isn't it, because it *isn't* a happy story. One friend of mine said he only read it at Lent because it was so hard and bitter." After another reviewer criticized his poetry as being simply bad, Tolkien replied that "a lot of the criticism of the verses shows a complete failure to understand the fact that they are all dramatic verses; they were conceived as the kind of things people would say under the circumstances." When Ballantine published a revised edition of *The Lord of the Rings* ten years after the original work was first reviewed, Tolkien used that opportunity to state in the introduction that "Some who have read the book, or at any rate have reviewed it, have found it boring, absurd, or contemptible; and I have no cause to complain, since I have similar opinions of their works, or the kinds of writing that they evidently prefer."

After being a professor for some 30 years, Tolkien finally began to win both recognition and reward for his academic achievements and scholarly contributions to English philology and literature. In 1954, he was awarded honorary Doctor of Letters (D.Litt.) by both University College in Dublin, Ireland, and the University of Liège in Belgium. The professor of English philology at the University of Liège was Professor d'Ardenne, who had once been Tolkien's star student at Oxford. Professor d'Ardenne undoubtedly played no small part in securing the honorary degree for his old friend and colleague.

Although Tolkien was nearing the end of a long and distinguished academic career, and his most important scholastic contributions had been made some years earlier, it was only in the 1950's that he came to be known outside his own field. In 1953, he was invited to deliver the William Paton Ker Memorial Lecture at the University of Glasgow in Scotland. Ker had been a famous medievalist, teacher, and poet; he had held several professorial chairs, including one at Oxford. After he died in 1923, the University of Glasgow established an annual lecture in his name, to be given by a distinguished scholar to an audience comprising scholars. Tolkien was accorded the honor of delivering the lecture on the eve of the publication of *The Lord of the Rings*. Another honor bestowed upon Tolkien was honorary membership in the *Hid Islezka bokmennta-félag*, an Icelandic society. And before his retirement, Tolkien was elected vice-president of the Philological Society of Great Britain. That the honors came so late in life was because Tolkien published so very little in the way of academic papers, texts, or reference books. It has been said that "Lewis published too much and Tolkien too little;" this is borne out by fellow Inkling and Oxford don C. L. Wrenn, who once told Professor Przemyslaw Mroczkowski that "Tolkien is a genius! If only he wrote accordingly, what wonders could he accomplish." It was gratifying to Tolkien that international recognition as a scholar came before his fame as a writer, and not the other way around.

The Tolkiens moved once more in 1954, at the time that *The Fellowship of the Ring* was first published. Their new house was in nearby Headington— a suburban town east of the city—which straddled the busy London road. When Tolkien was an undergraduate, Headington had been a mere village, but like other Oxford suburbs, it had grown to provide housing for workers at the Morris motor works in Cowley. Tolkien purchased a pleasant white house at 76 Sandfield Road, not far from where C. S. Lewis lived, and later, just down the street from W. H. Auden. Auden, by the way, did not like Tolkien's house. He told Richard Plotz, president of the Tolkien Society of America, that "he lives in a hideous house—I can't tell you how awful it is— with hideous pictures on the walls."

Ironically, the money with which Tolkien purchased the house came, not from the advance or royalties from *The Lord of the Rings*, but from the sale of the manuscript to Marquette University in Milwaukee, Wisconsin. When asked why he did so, Tolkien confessed "I wanted the money very badly to buy this house."

All the Tolkien children had grown up and branched off on their own. Christopher was a fellow at New College, Oxford, and a member of the English School as a lecturer in Old English. He lived in a rented house on

Holywell Street near his father's house on that street; incidentally, when John and Edith Tolkien moved to Headington, Christopher and his family took over Tolkien's rented house at 99 Holywell street. Michael Tolkien had left Oxford and become a teacher, and later, schoolmaster, at the Benedictine School in Ampleforth, Yorkshire. Priscilla Tolkien became a teacher at a technical college in Oxford (not associated with the University), and lived at the northernmost part of the city. The eldest, Father John Tolkien, was the Catholic chaplain at Keele University in Staffordshire, and also had a small parish in the district. John and Priscilla remained single; Christopher and Michael married and had families.

Tolkien greatly enjoyed having young children in his house once again. He delighted in playing with his grandchildren (who called him Grand*fellow*) whenever they came to Headington. Once when one of his grandsons was busy being overly rambunctious during a walk, Tolkien threatened the child that if he wasn't good, something black and terrible would come from the sky. At that instant, a truck driver lost control of his vehicle and swerved through a nearby hedge before crashing to a stop. The child was astonished and awe-struck at his grandfather's supposed magical powers, and while the story does not recount what happened afterwards, the lad probably mended his ways for a brief time. His was a happy household, and when the children came visiting, Tolkien amused them as he had his own a generation earlier by making up stories for them. He was a conventional grandfather, extremely proud of his sons' children, slightly doting, mildly indulging, and always respectful of them as human beings. Tolkien once said that he thought that "children aren't a class. They are merely human beings at different stages of maturity. All of them have a human intelligence which even at its lowest is a pretty wonderful thing, and the entire world in front of them." He was especially proud of his grandson, Michael George David Reuel Tolkien, a "demon chess player" who later studied English philology at Merton College.

Tolkien's grandchildren visited him more often than he visited them; his wife Edith was still in poor health and not up to casual social visits. In later years they became rather reclusive, staying at home for weeks at a time. Tolkien wished to travel now that he had the money, but with his wife's ill health and the high demands of his position at the English School, he found he had to stay at home. Thus, he was unable to accept an invitation to visit the United States in autumn, 1957, when both Harvard University and Marquette University wished to confer honorary degrees upon him. In response to the latter invitation, Tolkien wrote rather belatedly in May, 1957 that "I have ill repaid the generosity of Marquette by my discourtesy of silence. Without going into long details this has been due not to lack of pleasure (indeed excitement and delight) in the generous invitation, but to overwork, difficult domestic and academic circumstances, and the necessity of coping (or trying to cope) with a now very large mail, as well as heavy professional work and duties, without *any secretary!*" Later that year, he wrote in a letter that both health and an overloaded schedule were still plaguing him. He wrote, "I will not bother you with a long wail, but June and July are usually crowded months academically, and I have been much harassed. Also, I have not been well recently, and arthritic trouble with the right hand has been a hinderance. Fortunately the hand does not object to tapping keys as much as to a pen; but I prefer a pen."

The Inklings continued to meet, but rather sporadically after C. S. Lewis accepted the new chair in Medieval and Renaissance History at the University of Cambridge in 1954, as well as a fellowship at Magdalen College, Cambridge (no association with Magdalen College, Oxford). Lewis continued to live much of the time in Oxford, even after his marriage to Joy Davidman in 1957. He surrendered his life-long bachelorhood in a Christian act of charity, marrying a woman who was terminally ill with cancer; she lived on for three more years. Lewis himself was in poor health, and was about to relinquish his Cambridge chair when he died in 1963. His death ended what was left of the Inklings, and Tolkien lost his closest companion and most valued colleague as well.

The first edition of *The Lord of the Rings* not only sold out, but became an instant collector's item. Allen & Unwin issued another printing, and has continued to do so on a regular basis. Over the years, they have published limited editions, editions on India paper, paperback editions, one volume editions, boxed editions, and four-volume editions that include *The Hobbit*. By 1957, *The Lord of the Rings* had settled down to steady sales, and became a strong staple in both Allen & Unwin's and Houghton Mifflin's book catalogs.

Early on, the book had attracted the British Broadcasting Corporation, which had once dramatized *The Hobbit* on radio. In September, 1955, the BBC serialized *The Lord of the Rings* in ten parts for use in school broadcasts in the "Adventures in English" series. The BBC broadcast the programs to 27,697 schools throughout the British Isles, reaching upwards of 5 million children. Six years later, a 13-part dramatization of *The Lord of the Rings* was broadcast over BBC radio to the entire country; the cast included one of England's most popular radio actors, Bob Arnold, who regularly played the part of Tom Forrest in the long-running series *The Archers*. (Tolkien expressed interest in wanting to read *The Lord of the Rings* himself over the air, a suggestion wisely vetoed by the BBC.)

In 1957, Tolkien received, at the World Science Fiction convention held in London in that year, the first of many awards for his trilogy. The organization meets annually in different cities and gives awards for the best science fiction published the previous year. *The Lord of the Rings* was voted the best fantasy of 1956, and Tolkien was given his "Hugo" silver starship on September 10, 1957, by Miss Clemence Dame. During her presentation speech, Miss Dame said that "there is nothing in literature to rival it," and then ribbed the professor who "should be doing learned works" but instead wrote fantasy sagas. "But of course my answer is that it is a learned work," she hastily amended. To Tolkien the World Science Fiction award was something of a mixed blessing, since he said in his acceptance speech that "I have never written any science fiction." Ten years later, when a *New York Times* writer asked what he had done with the stainless steel sharp-finned rocket, he replied vaguely that "it's upstairs somewhere. It has fins. Quite different from what was required, as it turned out."

As is customary with famous people, Tolkien found himself deluged with requests to speak, lecture, or attend luncheons, dedications, and club meetings of all sorts. Most of the requests and invitations he turned down, claiming work and age; he also declined to be interviewed by journalists for some years, and only relented after *The Lord of the Rings* became a best-seller. One of the few invitations he was happy to accept was the dedication of the new Oxfordshire County Library on December 14, 1956. Books had always been important to his life, and he used the opportunity to reaffirm his belief in their increasing relevance to our society. "Books are besieged by a great many embattled enemies," he said, "but from them comes the food of the mind. It is not good for the stomach to be without food for a long period, and it is very much worse for the mind."

Tolkien's long and distinguished academic career was approaching its end; in 1958 he reached the mandatory retirement age. On the day before his 66th birthday, Merton College announced that they would bestow upon Tolkien an honorary fellowship, not because of his writings, but for service to the College, the University, and the many students whom Tolkien had influenced. Later, Exeter College followed suit and also elected Tolkien an honorary fellow. A year-and-a-half later, the Merton College Hall was packed for Tolkien's valedictory lecture. It was a strictly academic farewell in which Tolkien reflected some of the thoughts that he had voiced in his famous *Beowulf: The Monsters and the Critics* lecture 23 years earlier. He denounced the "old errors" and "deflating asides" by scholars who sometimes lose sight of their objectives, and rather than concentrate on reading the old sagas and epics, make "melodramatic declamations in Anglo-Saxon." His audience greeted his words with thunderous applause, a fitting climax to a brilliant career.

As Professor Emeritus, Tolkien continued his research in philology and Anglo-Saxon literature. He contributed to *Jerusalem Bible*, an interdenominational translation hailed by both scholars and theologians as one of the best ever. Tolkien was asked to translate the Book of Job into French, which he did with customary brilliance. In 1962, he published the text to the *Ancrene Wisse*, a religious treatise from the late 12th century; Tolkien probably collaborated with his former student, Professor d'Ardenne of the University of Liège, in the preparation of the text. Tolkien and d'Ardenne edited the text for the Early English Text Society, and it was published the same year by Oxford University Press. As late as 1967, Tolkien concerned himself with such matters. At that time he also finished a modern translation of his own edited text of *Sir Gawain and the Green Knight*. With the Sir Gawain translation was the translation of a poem called *The Pearl*; both were published by Oxford University Press.

By 1961 the excitement generated by *The Lord of the Rings* had quietly expanded from academics to science fiction addicts. Since news of the trilogy and mention of Professor Tolkien had all but disappeared from public view, some critics mistakenly concluded that *The Lord of the Rings* had been a flash-in-the-pan fad. The English critic Phillip Toynbee wrote in the London *Observer* that "there was a time when the Hobbit fantasies of Professor Tolkien were being taken very seriously indeed by a great many distinguished literary figures. Mr. Auden is even reported to have claimed that these books were as good as *War and Peace*; Edwin Muir and many others were almost equally enthusiastic. I had a sense that one side or the other must be mad, for it seemed to me that these books were dull, ill-written, whimsical and childish. And for me this had a reassuring outcome, for most of his more ardent supporters were soon beginning to sell out their shares in Professor Tolkien, and today [1961] those books have passed into merciful oblivion."

Perhaps it is difficult to appreciate now the intense controversy *The Lord of the Rings* at first stimulated. According to the critic R. J. Reilly, Tolkien's trilogy provoked on a modest scale the kind of critical controversy that had accompanied T. S. Eliot's *The Waste Land* and James Joyce's *Ulysses*. Literary critics could not *ignore* Tolkien and felt impelled either to support or to condemn his work. Colin Wilson gives an example of such divided loyalties in his essay *Tree by Tolkien*. In it he says that "a few years ago, I went to have lunch with W. H. Auden in his New York apartment. It was the first time I'd met him, and Norman Mailer had warned me that I might find him difficult to get along with. (Very reserved, very English—but more so than most Englishmen.) I found this true on the whole—he seemed to be very formal, perhaps basically shy. But after we had been eating for ten minutes, he asked me suddenly: 'Do you like *The Lord of the Rings*?' I said I thought it was a masterpiece. Auden smiled, 'I somehow thought you would.' The manner softened noticeably, and the lunch proceeded in a more relaxed atmosphere.

"It is true, as Peter S. Beagle remarked in his introduction to *The Tolkien Reader*, that Tolkien admirers form a sort of club. Donald Swann [who wrote the music for *Poems and Songs of Middle Earth* and became a friend of Tolkien's] is another member—but that is understandable, for his temperament is romantic and imaginative. It is harder to understand why someone as 'intellectual' as Auden should love Tolkien, while other highly intelligent people find him somehow revolting. (When I mentioned to a friend—who is an excellent critic—that I intended to write an essay on Tolkien, he said: 'Good, it's about time somebody exploded that bubble,' taking it completely for granted that it would be an attack.) Angus Wilson told me in 1956 that he thought that *The Lord of the Rings* was a 'don's whimsy' (although he may have changed his mind since then). . . ."

Nevertheless, Tolkien's books continued to sell well, and his publishers encouraged him to prepare a book of poetry from *The Lord of the Rings* for release in 1962. This he did with pleasure, since it promised more money and little exertion; after all, most of it had been written already, and only had to be selected and properly introduced. That book became *The Adventures of Tom Bombadil*. Allen & Unwin also encouraged Tolkien to write more about hobbits and Middle-earth, but Tolkien was primarily interested in returning to his earlier works in order to prepare them for publication. So it was that after more than 40 years, Tolkien took up again *The Silmarillion*, the "prequel" to *The Lord of the Rings*. This task was to continue to the end of his life.

One serious tactical mistake that Allen & Unwin made about *The Lord of the Rings* was in greatly underestimating its audience. The trilogy became an "underground" classic among science fiction and fantasy readers, many of whom could not afford $15 or more for a three-volume hardbound set. There had been a sizable paperback market for the work almost immediately after its initial publication in the mid-50s, but no paperback edition was forthcoming. This oversight by both Allen & Unwin and Houghton Mifflin created a vacuum that was filled by a less conservative publishing house, Ace Books.

There is still considerable difference of opinion about the "great copyright controversy" over the American edition of *The Lord of the Rings*. The only thing absolutely established is that the original edition of *The Lord of the Rings* is *not* copyrighted in the United States, and is therefore in the public domain (which means that any publishing house can issue it without having to pay royalties to Tolkien's heirs). According to Houghton Mifflin's version, the complicated and confusing American copyright law is really to blame. They claim that before America joined the International Copyright Convention, there had been various subsections of the law designed to protect the American printing industry. One was known as the "manufacturing clause," and it stated that a publisher would fail to establish American copyright if he imported more than 1,445 printed copies of a book from a foreign country. Houghton Mifflin supposedly imported small numbers of *The Lord of the Rings* at first, but when sales, and therefore demand, picked up, they ordered more and more until they inadvertently exceeded the maximum limit by 555. The "restrictive and controversial" law automatically went into force, and copyright was therefore never established.

On the other hand, Donald Wollheim, who was chief editor of Ace Books at the time that Ace brought out an uncopyrighted edition of *The Lord of the Rings*, lays responsibility at Houghton Mifflin's door. "They figured that it would only sell 500 copies or less in this country, so they imported sheets and didn't bother to copyright it. Afterwards, they couldn't sell it to a paperback house under any circumstances because it had no copyright, and if it hadn't been for someone like Ace, *The Lord of the Rings* wouldn't be in paperback to this very day.

"It was very easy to see that the original edition was in the public domain because it carries no copyright; that is the simple situation. English copyright law is quite different from American copyright law; American copyright law requires that a book should carry a statement on the page following the title page: Copyright (the date of publication), By (the name of the copyright owner). In England, this is not required. When an American publisher imports printed sheets from England and binds them here under his own imprint, he must either overprint the Copyright, or else take out an *ad interim* copyright that would give him 18 months in which to print an American edition or lose copyright. But if you place a book on sale without a copyright notice, it falls into the public domain immediately, according to United States copyright law. The original Houghton Mifflin edition is in the public domain, and anyone can print it without asking permission or paying royalties.

"What they did after we published the Ace edition was to get Professor Tolkien to revise the book, making little changes here and there, and that's what their copyright really covers: only slight revisions."

Ace Books was and still is a major paperback publisher of popular science fiction (and were distinguished as such for many years because of their usually lurid covers and cheap prices). Wollheim, who specializes in science fiction, knew about the underground popularity of *The Lord of the Rings* and wanted to get the rights to publish it in paperback for Ace Books. He quickly found out that the trilogy was not copyrighted in the United

States, and therefore began (according to him) lengthy and frustrating negotiations with Professor Tolkien through Allen & Unwin. Allen & Unwin was unenthusiastic, and Tolkien did not respond at all. When Wollheim finally advised his publisher, A. A. Wyn, of the situation, Wyn told him that since the trilogy was in the public domain, he should go ahead and publish it. The Ace Books edition (minus the appendices), with suitably sensational covers, went on sale in May, 1965.

Allen & Unwin became aware of the imminent publication of the Ace Books edition, and decided to counter it by bringing out an "authorized" paperback edition of their own. Ballantine Books was selected to publish the work in paperback, not so much because of its already established fantasy series (edited by Lin Carter), but because Houghton Mifflin apparently had a considerable financial investment in Ballantine. They persuaded Tolkien to make various changes in the main text, add information to the appendices, and write a completely new introduction to *The Lord of the Rings*. (In addition, the edition would carry a forward by the American writer Peter S. Beagle.) Tolkien wrote the introduction with some enthusiasm, since it gave him an opportunity to make various corrections of unintentional errors that he, and other perceptive readers, had noted.

The Ace edition beat the Ballantine edition into print by almost five months, during which time the initial printing of 50,000 completely sold out; within a year (during which time it competed against the Ballantine edition) the Ace edition managed to sell an additional 150,000 complete copies of the trilogy, and this despite the fact that it had neither index nor appendices, but rather, bad publicity and considerable criticism; but the Ace edition was also more than a dollar cheaper than the Ballantine edition.

Raynor Unwin condemned Ace's action as "moral piracy," but took no legal action since none was possible. Tolkien himself was publicly indignant, and states in the Ballantine edition that "I hope that those who have read *The Lord of the Rings* with pleasure will not think me ungrateful: to please readers was my main object, and to be assured of this has been a great reward. Nonetheless, for all its defects of omission and inclusion, it was the product of long labor, and like a simple-minded hobbit I feel that it is, while I am still alive, my property in justice unaffected by copyright laws. It seems to me a grave discourtesy, to say no more, to issue my book without even a polite note informing me of the project: dealings one might expect of Saruman in his decay rather than from the defenders of the West. However that may be, this paperback edition and no other has been published with my consent and cooperation. Those who approve of courtesy (at least) to living authors will purchase it and no other. And if the many kind readers who have encouraged me with their letters will add to

their courtesy by referring friends or enquirers to Ballantine Books, I shall
be very grateful. To them, and to all who have been pleased by this book,
especially those Across the Water for whom it is specially intended, I
dedicate this volume." But in December, 1965, he relented slightly by
admitting that "However, there has been a great fuss in the press and on
television about this piracy, and it all adds up to rather good advertisement
for my work."

Ace's publishing the work in paperback was probably the best thing
that ever happened to Tolkien. In a word, it "took off like a rocket"
(according to Donald Wollheim's wife), revealing the unrealized readership
potential for an affordable edition of *The Lord of the Rings*. Despite the
official acrimony and the charge of moral piracy, Tolkien profited
handsomely from the entire affair. Technically, Ace Books didn't have to
give Tolkien a single penny for the rights to his books, but A. A. Wyn
decided to set aside all the money that would have ordinarily gone to the
author and establish a Tolkien Prize, which would encourage young writers
of science fiction and fantasy. When Wollheim wrote to Tolkien of their
intention to apply the $11,000 that would have gone in royalties to a
literary prize in his name, Tolkien responded and asked for the money
himself. Since the agreement was between Ace and Tolkien, the entire
$11,000 went directly to the Professor. Ordinarily the author and original
publisher share 50-50 in any foreign rights; with three publishers—Allen &
Unwin, Houghton Mifflin, and Ballantine Books—this meant that Tolkien
received only 25% of the royalties from the official American edition. Since
no other publishers were involved with Ace, Tolkien received 100%. It is
likely that Tolkien publicly denied any knowledge of Ace's intention prior
to publication because he did not wish either to anger or to embarrass his
own publishers by going behind their backs in a technically legal but
ethically questionable maneuver. On the other hand, Tolkien knew that
Houghton Mifflin had muffed the American copyright through negligence,
and possibly felt little loyalty to them at the time and also justified in taking
all the money for himself. After Ace Books paid Professor Tolkien all the
royalties due him, they received a letter from him expressing his
satisfaction with the outcome. Ace, stung from adverse publicity, a boycott
of their edition, and continuing acrimony with Tolkien's other publishers,
announced that once the current edition went out of print, they would not
issue more.

By the end of 1965, *The Lord of the Rings* had become a dramatic best-
seller both in England and in America. Tolkien was propelled from relative
obscurity to world-wide fame; till then, his works had brought him only
modest affluence, but now they promised the comfortable wealth that had

eluded him all his life. But the price he was to pay for popular success was one he could not easily afford: the loss of privacy. To a man like Tolkien, the celebrity status that the public insisted on according him robbed him of time, peace of mind, and the ability to work unhindered on his remaining life's work, *The Silmarillion*. To Tolkien, success turned out to be a terrible two-edged sword.

TIMOTHY R. O'NEILL

The Individuated Hobbit

Bilbo Baggins of Bag End was as conventional a hobbit as any other—despite the influence of his scandalous mother—and, like his conservative associates, eschewed adventure in all its distasteful forms. The most dangerous adventure of all, of course, is the journey into one's own psyche; and it is just that adventure that Bilbo undertakes in the fiftieth year of his life.

Nor is he really dragged kicking and screaming by the wizard and thirteen Dwarves. As they sang of the silence and majesty, the gleaming crystal columns and torchlit halls of the Lonely Mountain, Bilbo felt a stirring in his heart:

> Then something Tookish woke up inside him, and he wished to go and see the great mountains, and hear the pine-trees and the waterfalls, and explore the caves, and wear a sword instead of a walking stick.

But this glimpse of the shadow world, the sudden revealing of a forgotten strain of Tookishness, is too much for this watchful, timid hobbit consciousness:

From *The Individuated Hobbit: Jung, Tolkien and the Archetypes of Middle-earth* by Timothy R. O'Neill. © 1979 by Timothy R. O'Neill.

Suddenly in the wood beyond The Water a flame leapt up—
probably somebody lighting a wood fire—and he thought of
plundering dragons settling on his quiet Hill and kindling it all
to flames. He shuddered; and very quickly he was plain Mr.
Baggins of Bag End, Under-Hill, again.

The potency of these newly awakened symbols is so compelling that Bilbo
must suppress the strange and disquieting feelings they evoke, unbidden,
from the depths of what serves a hobbit for an unconscious. The
Tookishness subsides.

This "Tookishness" is explicitly personified as the "fabulous
Belladonna Took," Bilbo's mother. It is a female figure; a magical, potent
figure out of Faërie, and the author and manipulator of his urges to climb
above his humdrum hobbit existence. It is also his link with the collective
past—the narrator speculates that some hobbit in the Took genealogy must
have taken a fairy (Elvish) wife, another reference to the mystical and
reverential, dimensions quite foreign to hobbit affairs. This is the first
inkling that Bilbo is about to break out of his one-sided life, and it frightens
him. Well it might, for even in the brave departure from the Shire,
"running as fast as his furry feet could carry him," he could not have
guessed what horrors lay ahead. How many hobbits of his generation had
been obliged to deal with trolls, or seen trolls, or even believed in them?
Only Bilbo, one presumes.

And fearsome trolls they are. Bilbo's world is a dream world, a Faërie
world; and in the world of dreams, of the psyche, the aggressive animal may
symbolize unrestrained libido. The trolls, although nominally
anthropomorphic, seem to fall into this functional category—if there was
ever inarticulate, unrestrained libido in action, it is the trio of Bert, Bill,
and Tom. This may be regarded as the first sign of the power, the
numinous potency, of the complexes that reside in Bilbo's unconscious.

Gandalf serves here as rescuer, but he is much more than that; I have
reserved a separate chapter for this amazing personage. For now, he is the
guide, good for an occasional flash of temper and magic. Later on he will
serve a more dramatic purpose—his powers will mature.

The travelers' brief respite in Rivendell allows the interpretation of
Thorin's map, and the secrets hidden in it by magic are revealed by Elrond.
Elrond is a symbol of the union of opposites (Elf and Man); it is only
logical that he should be the one to find the key to the map—the moon-
letters, runes that are revealed only by moonlight. He brings forth the
hidden instructions ("stand by the grey stone when the thrush knocks")
from the depths of the unconscious, the clue which will unlock the secrets

of the hidden psyche. The moon is often connected, at least in the male psyche, with the unconscious, as the sun may symbolize in men's dreams and imagination the conscious.

After their departure from Rivendell, wizard, Dwarves, and hobbit are confronted by a mountain storm; the sudden fury and flashes of lightning portend symbolically the approach of a sudden psychic change, and the change which is about to occur is the most dramatic and significant of all.

Bilbo's progress thus far has only hinted at the coming crisis, the first stirrings of a change that may express the symptoms of neurosis; but this is not the real psyche, only a dream psyche. The appearance of certain portents, numinous images charged with inflated power that surge from the depths of the unconscious, serve as warnings—warnings that invariably make Bilbo long for the solid comfort of his hobbit-hole. The last thing Mr. Baggins wants to undertake at this point is a journey Under Hill into the depths of his forgotten mind and a confrontation with the unlovely demons of the imagination that lurk there. Attention is reversed now, from an outward to an inward perspective, and the frightful fiend is thus ahead rather than behind. But with thirteen dwarves pulling him on and a wizard standing rear guard to head off any thoughts of malingering, Bilbo must march on.

Descent may symbolize the direction of attention and energy into the unconscious, and this is where Bilbo is dumped unceremoniously during the party's headlong flight from the pursuing mountain goblins. Lost and alone, he stumbles exhausted, and his hand finds—by chance?—the Ring.

Imagine yourself groping blindly about the darkness of your own unconscious, uncertain of what direction to take. Directing your efforts is *you*, as you know yourself—the ego complex. But the ego is conscious, and is treading unfamiliar paths. You are only dimly aware now, after signals granted you in dream and vision, of the presence of another *you*—forgotten, ignored, reflexively denied, buried far from the light of day. It is both you and not-you, noman and everyman, your constant companion on the foggy road.

"Deep down here by the dark water lived old Gollum, a small slimy creature." Tolkien professes ignorance of Gollum's origins in *The Hobbit*. But we shall learn later that old Gollum is, or was, Sméagol, a hobbit who dwelt ages ago by the banks of the Great River. The very idea is repulsive to Frodo when he first hears of it, years later: "How loathsome! . . . I can't believe that Gollum was connected with hobbits, however distantly . . . what an abominable notion!" Heretofore Gollum was only a slimy, unlovely curiosity; now he is much more threatening, the image of the nightmare not-hobbit, the alter ego that lurks just out of sight.

Gollum paddles about his little cold pool of water deep at the mountain's roots. The deep water is associated symbolically with the unconscious, with depth and knowledge and wisdom. Bilbo's progress has thus been *descent* into the *unconscious*, in the first timid search for enlightenment. But true wisdom for Bilbo must be shunted aside—the first order of business is to get out of that mountain as soon as possible. The revelations of the unconscious are really too much! The key to escape is slimy old Gollum, repulsive though he may be. Their riddle game is a duel of conscious and unconscious preoccupations. Bilbo marshals images of an egg (symbolizing the eye of the conscious), eating (material world), sun on the daisies (*sol* as representation of the conscious); Gollum relies upon contrasting pictures: wind, darkness, the roots of mountains, fish. But Bilbo is careless and fated to be anything but rid of Gollum, whatever the outcome of the riddle game. He gives Gollum his *name*—an important piece of information not to be blurted heedlessly to anyone, much less a mildewy green-eyed figure of shadow who lives in a cave, eats raw goblins caught unawares, and talks to himself. And Bilbo, above all, has the Ring, in whose shining symmetry is encased Gollum's dark soul.

No, Bilbo is never free of Gollum, and never quite breaks away from that riddle game under the mountain. Symbolically this is the pivot point of the story, and the most powerful juxtaposition of forces. It clearly moved the author, since Tolkien was never quite content to leave this haunting episode behind until it had been elaborated and resolved many years and three volumes later. In the Jungian sense, this is a confrontation of immense potential, so much that it has enthralled countless readers, fascinated by its stark primordial imagery and the sympathetic chord in the readers' collective soul.

Bilbo is clearly the ego, as the focal personality thus far in the story. More than this, Bilbo is the reader's ego. Bilbo's adventure has become the reader's dream, his creative, vicarious inner experience. The ego has courageously (more or less) entered the forbidden recesses of the unconscious and collided unexpectedly with its dark mirror image. The collision is brief and incomplete—the two are now for the first time fully aware of each other's existence, and their fates are inseparably bound. The only possible end of this dream lies many years and many miles ahead, at the Cracks of Doom.

Ego and shadow face each other at the twilit border of dark and light, and they are tied together by a precious ring, the One Ring, the "One Ring to find them/One Ring to bring them all and in the darkness bind them."

This is the ruling Ring, for it rules both their fates; and these fates are bound, as is foretold, "in the Land of Mordor where the Shadows lie."

We have already noted in the previous chapter on Jungian theory that individuation and Self-realization are not achieved by the conquest and destruction of the shadow. Only more one-sidedness is at the close of that battle, for the shadow is a necessary part of the psyche, the source of creativity as well as darker impulse. Old Gollum, in any case, for all his gulping evil unwholesome ruminations, cowardice, and endless autistic self-pity, is not all bad. Years later, Gandalf parries Frodo's instinctive revulsion and vindictiveness:

> He had proved tougher than even one of the Wise could have guessed—as a hobbit might. There was a little corner of his mind that was still his own, and light came through it, as through a chink in the dark: a light out of the past.

But Frodo needs a lot of convincing. Gollum is still part of the picture, and he can never be brushed aside without endangering the preordained balance of the psyche. It is clear at least to the perceptive that Gollum has a role to play in the coming drama. I personally find Gollum one of the most sympathetic figures in the story. He is indeed a key actor in the play, and it may not be fair to cast him in a role of shadow. It might be just as accurate to call him an ego dominated by dark impulse but finally capable of being driven in desperation to some slender virtue or hair-raising vice as the scenario dictates, just as Bilbo and Frodo are ego personifications easily inclined to the light but ever aware of the dark shadow vestige which may emerge at critical moments. Bilbo is capable of spinning tall tales about his "precious" just as Gollum does, without thinking. And Frodo, everyone's hero, really fails the test at the dramatic moment, and must be rescued by his slithering, unwilling shadow.

I am, of course, dancing lightly about the truly central (literally and figuratively) issue of the Ring. The Ring is the focal point of the symbolic story, and as such subtly overwhelms the overt plot like the latent content of a dream that belies the manifest experience. To say that either *The Hobbit* or *The Lord of the Rings* is a tale of there and back again is to suggest that the *Divine Comedy* is a book about cave exploring. Tolkien's faërie world is a world of light and dark, a realm with very few softer tones (and whenever a character seems to assume a mantle of grey ambivalence, the cause is invariably the Ring). At the border is the twilight, the furthest marches of the conscious, where things are not as they seem: and binding these realms together is the precious Ring.

The Ring is perfect in form, and stands for the Self—the Ruling Ring, that is to say, is the way in which the archetype of the Self-in-potentia personifies itself. Critics have compared the Ring to Andvari's treasure in *der Ring des Nibelungen*. This is an interesting comparison, but falls short of the essential symbolic contribution of the precious.

The Ring's symmetry is perfectly balanced, a graceful circle, distilling the concepts of balance and perfection and the union of all opposites that will characterize the Self after its realization. Its material is gold, because of its incorruptible nature as in the philosophy of alchemy. Jung was fascinated by the complex and powerful imagery of medieval alchemy and the theology of the proto-Christian Gnostics, and we will examine the appearance of a variety of symbolic conventions from these sources. He believed that the alchemic and Gnostic symbolic sources, with their recognition of the importance of balance, opposition, and compensation, were psychologically more satisfying than the meager imagery of Protestantism in particular or western Christianity in general. In any case, the form and function of the Ring are not left in doubt. The Ring's fate is etched inside and out in fiery letters:

> *One Ring to rule them all, One Ring to find them.*
> *One Ring to bring them all and in the darkness bind them.*

The Ring is the Self, the potential force that promises finally to make whole both hobbit and Middle-earth.

But Bilbo is not through spelunking—ahead lie the Lonely Mountain and a far more formidable foe than wretched Gollum. Bilbo must now earn his title of burglar—or "expert treasure-hunter," as he would doubtless prefer to be called—by dickering with Smaug the Mighty, "greatest and chiefest of catastrophes."

The dragon is a common symbol in the mythologies of a variety of times and cultures. In form, it is a fusion of serpent, bird, and other animals, and I cannot resist digressing for a few paragraphs in honor of this fantastic beast and its importance in understanding the imagery of the psyche.

The winged snake is encountered in odd places. The medical profession in this country has embraced the caduceus as its symbol. This is actually an error—the proper symbol, and that which is used elsewhere, is the staff of Asklepios, a stick about which is entwined the single serpent. I shall not bother with the mythological basis for this emblem, since it does not influence our present concerns; but the caduceus, whether it is appropriate for the medical profession or not, gives us a hint about winged snakes in general.

The caduceus is the winged staff of Hermes, the Greek god who served as messenger and patron of travelers. He is also the intermediary between gods and the underworld; unifier of light and darkness, his common symbol being the phallic *herm* placed at crossroads. He is also the guide of dead souls, which is not encouraging for patients whose doctors embrace his staff. The symbolic nature of the caduceus is fairly straightforward: the serpents are chthonic, earthy, close to the underworld, suggestive of Man's lowly phylogenetic origins. The wings reflect the soaring soul of Man, the consciousness that sets him apart from his scaly and furry forefathers. The central staff binds the two together—mating snakes, the instinctual substrate, flying bird, the sunlit potential of consciousness.

The union of opposites is thus an essential part of such figures, among which we must place the dragon. Those familiar with mythology will point out that the Serpent of Midgard, who gnawed for ages at the roots of the Norse world tree Yggdrasil, was a "worm": creeping and wingless. Remember, however, that he was compensated (as was the rest of the complex Norse world) by the eagle that perched in the top branches of the tree. The two symbols are not yet fused, and carry on no more than a spirited dialogue through the good offices of a squirrel whose fate it is to scamper up and down Yggdrasil's loftiness from one to the other until the day of Ragnarökk.

But Smaug the Mighty is a full-fledged (should one say "fledged"? His wings are batlike and featherless) fire-drake, long of tooth, broad of wing, bad of breath, and shudderingly articulate.

Tolkien, for some reason which will remain unguessed, was very nonevaluative in his general treatment of dragons. The worms of *The Silmarillion* are a pretty grim lot, true; but then there is little frivolity about that work, composed of the tear-soaked chronicles of the Eldar's trials in Middle-earth. I have already made clear to the reader that I am not impressed by the Elves' studious garment-rending and hand-wringing. Had they bothered to stop and talk for a few moments with any of the dragons set against them, they might have found entertainment enough to offset the confounded eternal weariness of the world. When Tolkien removes his Elvish persona and confronts dragons as the plucky hobbit or the sturdy yeoman-farmer, worms fare better. *Chrysophylax Dives* is merely living up to his miserly name, and doing so with wit, gusto, and a pinch of pathos. Smaug is certainly not to be trifled with, and admittedly dealt rather summarily with the Dwarves in the time of Thrain; but he is older now and perceptibly more mellow, at least willing to chat for a while before belching napalm and ending meaningful dialogue. And if he is greedy, well, that is what dragons are supposed to be; we cannot blame him for that, nor expect altruism of a fire-drake any more than empathy from a weeping crocodile. I really find Smaug altogether more worthy of sympathy than some hobbits—Lobelia Sackville-Baggins would have smitten the pesky lizard with a furled umbrella and sent him off whimpering. But perhaps after all pestiferous and acquisitive relatives are more likely to interrupt our serenity in contemporary times than thundering dragons.

Bilbo is terrified. Sting and Ring are hardly more than lucky charms in the great treasure cave, not proof against the fearful flamethrower. Smaug is what we of Othello's trade call an area weapon: precise location of the target is not required, nor is fastidious marksmanship necessary for good terminal effect. But Bilbo has guts that belie his species' reputation. None of the Dwarves, not even the venerable, much-decorated Thorin Oakenshield, who proved his mettle in the Goblin Wars, has volunteered to help him burgle treasure with the dragon so near. As he treads the tunnel coming ever nearer to the uninviting red glow the "least Tookish part of him" wavers, wishing yet again for the comfy hole at Bag End.

This is the persona (the "good decent hobbit") railing impotently at the anima (the Tookish part, personified as the great Belladonna, from whom he has surely inherited the propensity for disturbing sleeping dragons); but the objections are too little and much too late. He is committed to the path of Self-realization, like it or not. In fact, the controlled social mask is already slipping away, no longer supported by the need to maintain a reputation for the neighbors.

The nature of Bilbo's journey across the landscape of the psyche is revealed by his reply to Smaug's inquiry: "Who are you and where do you come from, if I may ask?"

> "You may indeed! I come from under the hill, and under the hills and over the hills my paths led. And through the air. I am he that walks unseen."

Over hill and under hill, indeed; Bilbo is too modest (if that is possible). "I am the friend of bears [a reference to Beorn, the theriomorphic figure we will discuss in more detail later] and the guest of eagles. I am Ringwinner and Luckwearer . . .

This is a complex and pregnant sort of name. It traces his path through conscious and unconscious (over hill and under hill) that has led him this far; establishes his foundation in both worlds ("friend of bears"—i.e., chthonic, earthy, bound to the animal shadow, the instinctive foundation of the psyche; and "guest of eagles"—one who may also soar at will in the light of consciousness). He glories in his new position as pivotal figure in the drama, the link between worlds (Ringwinner) and the key to fortune (Luckwearer) by possession of the magical transcending treasure.

But Bilbo succumbs to a near fatal weakness at this critical point. He has in the euphoria of the moment reveled too thoughtlessly in Belladonna's triumph, ignored the conscious part of him, which would have been more cautious and circumspect in talking to dragons. Smaug is sure-footed in the dark world, he has dwelt there long; Bilbo is a stranger in the perilous realm, and he has barely stepped into it before the incautious foot is thrust in his mouth, tipping off the worm to dangerous details of the plan. "*Thief* in the *Shadows!*" snarls the beast, "my armour is like tenfold shields, my teeth are swords, my claws spears, the shock of my tail a thunderbolt, my wings a hurricane, and my breath death!"

This uncouth outburst is one that reveals the volume and fury of the long-repressed libido, the surging, powerful energy that has for so long been denied conscious symbolization. Smaug has for the moment ceased to be a transcendental, transforming symbol and become pure animal power, untamed psychic drive. But transforming symbol is his major role still, the winged serpent, and like St. George, Bilbo must slay or outwit the beast to pave the way for the Self's advent. He has already done this, though he has no way of knowing it, with his careless clues—Smaug is soon up and around for the first time in years, and Bilbo has provided the clue through the help of the magic thrush that allows Bard the Bowman to finish the monster and quench his flames. The black arrow pierces the gap in Smaug's armor, and the treasure is now lying unguarded in the darkness under the mountain.

Now, as Bilbo and the Dwarves begin their greedy inventory of the reclaimed wealth, there is a significant discovery. Bilbo, unknown to Thorin and company, has found the Arkenstone, Heart of the Mountain. "Indeed there could not be two such gems, even in so marvellous a hoard, even in all the world." It is a perfect crystalline gem, a sparkling pale globe of light, the most cherished heirloom of the Dwarves of Erebor.

It is related in symbolism to the *lapis philosphorum*, the Philosopher's Stone of alchemy, which contains within its perfect symmetry the means of unifying the opposites, and means of transforming base metals into gold (also a union of opposites). In Jungian terms, it is a symbolic realization of the Self through individuation:

> The goal of individuation, as pictured in unconscious images, represents a kind of mid-point or center in which the supreme value and the greatest life-intensity are concentrated. It cannot be distinguished from images of the supreme values of the various religions. It appears as naturally in the individuation process as it does in the religions . . . a four-square city or garden . . . as the *imago Dei* in the soul, as the "circle whose

periphery is nowhere and whose center is everywhere," as a crystal, a stone, a tree, a vessel or a cosmic order . . .

Certainly its location, deep in the treasure cave at the mountain's roots, suggests its abode in the unconscious. Now it is more than a potential: it, like the Ring, is in Bilbo's "pocketses."

It does not remain there long, of course, and Bilbo uses this barter to resolve the political impasse between the Elves and Lakemen on one side and the Dwarves, "under bewilderment of the treasure," on the other. The Arkenstone is both symbol and instrument of his new-found Self; he blends now the pragmatic hobbit of the Shire with the courage and vision of the Tookish adventurer.

Indeed, the little burglar has retrieved more from the dragon's hoard than golden chalices and glittering jewels; his treasure is the treasure of the Self, beside which the wealth of the King under the Mountain, the splendor and worldly pomp and lucre are small change. At the last he has no use for more of this gold than his small measure—enough to be a well-to-do hobbit and live out his life in comfort and contemplation at Bag End (or so he believes). Bilbo Baggins will never be the same. The prosaic gentlehobbit is now poetic as well, his stuffy constricting persona shed (and Old Belladonna silenced), and the realization of his full potential within reach.

"My dear Bilbo!" observes Gandalf. "Something is the matter with you! You are not the hobbit that you were."

ANNE C. PETTY

Tolkien's Prelude

Frequently discussions of the creative fiction of Tolkien center around the trilogy only, often disregarding *The Hobbit* entirely. Although we may admit this slim volume was, in 1936, a single piece composed by Professor Tolkien to entertain his children, the use it served later in his developing conception of the history of the Third Age is indisputable. For this reason, any serious study of the fictive world of Tolkien must cast a discerning eye upon the original tale of hobbits as an interesting and necessary prelude to the grander work of *LOTR*. The most important demonstration we may conduct here in examining *The Hobbit* is the preliminary use of the folkloristic-mythic structures and functions that make up the intricate fabric of the trilogy. Granted the original hobbit tale superficially appears to be a more comical than serious quest; yet the most profound and ominous elements of *LOTR* are quarried from the foundations of this seemingly lighthearted tale of peril and adventure on the part of a bumbling amateur burglar. The reader should take careful note of the motivations and methods of transition operating within *The Hobbit*, for these are the same techniques employed in the trilogy in a much more complex, accomplished manner.

The Hobbit comfortably follows the three-stage quest of the hero delineated earlier, even though we are more inclined to see Bilbo as a comic figure, even the fool, rather than the hero of the quest. As the opening pages

From *One Ring To Bind Them All: Tolkien's Mythology* by Anne C. Petty. © 1979 by The University of Alabama Press.

unfold the nature of the quest to reader and fear-stricken hobbit alike, Gandalf the Wizard appears the more likely candidate for hero of the undertaking. This is a deliberate red herring, as we discover when we look closely at the developing hero consciousness in Bilbo, a crucial technique, for it is used again with added dimension in the characterization of Frodo in *LOTR*. We, like Bilbo and Frodo, are not cognizant of their heroic capabilities in the beginning. These qualities develop gradually before our eyes and theirs. Thus while we smile at them as hobbits, we seriously accept their heroic development and the magic surrounding it. Tolkien himself explains this approach in his essay, "On Fairy-stories": "There is one proviso: if there is any satire present in the tale, one thing must not be made fun of, the magic itself. That must in that story be taken seriously, neither laughed at nor explained away."

Tied closely to the developing hero personality in Bilbo as well as Gandalf is this concept of magic. For magic in Tolkien's terms does not mean any cheap, artificial, or external display of trickery and deception, but rather an immanent power of nature that men have somehow lost the ability to tap, presumably forever. Consequently the "magic" of the elves and wizards in both *The Hobbit* and *LOTR* is magic "of a peculiar mood and power, at the furthest pole from the vulgar devices of the laborious, scientific, magician." This understanding of the nature of Faerie prompts Tolkien to look upon the elves as far more "natural" than men, who are "supernatural" if anything, now that they have lost contact with the immanent power of the natural world. Bilbo the hobbit, of a race possessing "natural" magic that enables them to "disappear quietly and quickly when large stupid folk like you and me come blundering along," is not such an unlikely choice after all as key member of the quest company, as Gandalf well knew.

In the *Departure* segment of the tale we easily identify the elements of call to adventure, refusal of the call and subsequent acceptance, supernatural aid, and crossing the first threshold (corresponding to Vladimir Propp's functions of initial situation, negative and then positive reactions of the hero to persuasion, donor and magical agents, and dispatch of the hero from home). In this preliminary working of the mythic-quest pattern, Tolkien designates the frame of the tale as an "adventure" rather than a "quest," indicative of his still embryonic vision of the events of the Third Age. Yet the simple tale already possesses the mythic structure necessary for the difficult task of mythmaking (Tolkien's term for it is *subcreation*) as the subtitle of the book suggests: "There and Back Again."

The initial situation is located in the land called Hobbiton, where the reader is introduced to a single hobbit whose domestic well-being is about to be interrupted by a subtly veiled interdiction and prophecy. The initial iteration of the call to adventure comes from Gandalf as he interrupts the hobbit's morning smoke in the sun: "I am looking for someone to share in an adventure that I am arranging, and it's very difficult to find anyone." Bilbo's refusal of the call is worded with all the finality he can manage, "We don't want any adventures here, thank you!" Yet the subconscious acceptance of the call is there already, evident in Bilbo's excitement over the identity of the stranger and his notorious feats of magic. In answer to this unspoken receptivity, Gandalf makes the pronouncement that sets Bilbo on the road of the quest, "In fact I will go so far as to send you on this adventure," to which he adds a talisman insuring Bilbo's function as the seeker. With his wizard's staff Gandalf scratches a mysterious rune on the hobbit's tightly closed door. Bilbo's hurried invitation to tea the next day, although intended to get rid of the wizard momentarily, is yet another unconscious acceptance. Bilbo's actual overt response to the call is brought about by the persuasion of a magical agent: Thorin plays upon the golden harp of the dwarves and "Bilbo forgot everything else, and was swept away into dark lands under strange moons, far over The Water and very far from his hobbit-hole under The Hill."

A final observation on this point supplies another instance of the way in which the structural and folkloristic elements at work in this simple tale are carried over into the larger work of the trilogy; the hero must make an official statement of acceptance of the quest (in Propp, this is the beginning of the complication, the conjunctive moment containing the form of the hero's consent, and followed by the form of his dispatch in which the details of the quest are made known to him, including the phenomena to accompany him in the form of magical aids or equipment for the journey). In return for the official assent from the chosen hero, a donor, in this case Gandalf (a function trebled in the figures of Elrond and Beorn; trebling is an important structural device common to mythology and folklore), will bestow upon the hero aids either of a tangible or intangible nature. Bilbo's words "Tell me what you want done, and I will try it" serve as paradigm for the words Frodo is to speak on a fateful night in late October many years in the future.

Both receive magical aids, in Bilbo's case the map of Thror and his silver key to the secret back entrance into the Lonely Mountain. Also in return for the agreement to undertake the task, the hero is instructed in the nature of the quest, what the object sought for may be, and specifically what conduct is expected of the hero. Gandalf and Thorin explain to the overexcited hobbit, in persuasive terms that lure him, frighten him, and finally shame him into wanting to accompany the troupe of dwarves, that the dwarves are on a quest to regain their lost kingdom and treasure in the once-great dwarf city under the Lonely Mountain, now occupied by a "wicked worm," Smaug the Terrible. The expedition is badly in need, Gandalf has assured the dwarves, of a first-class burglar who will know how to extricate the treasure from the claws of the dragon, once he has also figured out how to slip into the ruins of the dwarf kingdom under the mountain.

Thus far we have the initial situation and preparatory section revealed in structural terms of the folkloristic functions. This analysis began with the situation of Bilbo enjoying his prosperity, safe and secure in Hobbiton before the "nasty adventure" presented itself on his doorstep. As Propp explains, ". . . the initial situation often presents a picture of unusual, sometimes emphasized, prosperity, often in quite vivid, beautiful forms. This prosperity serves as a contrasting background for the ensuing misfortune." We have learned that the only function obligatory to the folkloristic-mythic structure is the function (A) Villainy or (a) Lack; in *The Hobbit* the first function is (a^2) Lack of Wondrous Objects, for the dwarves have a great lack in that they are deprived of kingdom and treasure. This function also serves as motivation for the journey of the hero and master burglar; he is promised his share of the wealth, which he may choose himself. Following the explanation of the lack, the connective incident appears in the form of dispatch and lament (B^4): the dwarves' lay of their lost treasure enchants Bilbo momentarily and causes him to agree to join their cause. Immediately following is the sequence (DEF): the donor (Gandalf) presents the company with the map and key, the hero accepts these aids, and the magical agents are transferred from the donor to the head of the expedition, in this case Thorin, although it is the burglar's job to find out how to use them. The final function of this preparatory section is (G^4) Transference or Guidance to a Designated Place, in which the route to the Lonely Mountain is shown to Bilbo and the dwarves. From this point begins the first "move" or series of functions clustered around an act of villainy; each new (A) or (a) creates a new move, which accounts not only for the seemingly complicated tangle of events in *LOTR*, but as well for its artistically striking balance and symmetry in the simultaneous handling of the various plot lines.

A more modest version of this series occurs in *The Hobbit*, which does not contain the complex juxtaposition of moves traceable in *LOTR*. Fairly simple examples of repetition in moves occur here, which is to say that each act of villainy provides a parallel or paradigm for those that follow, emphasizing the height of the final villainy to which the tale ultimately ascends. Repetition on a more minute level has already occurred in the preparatory section, through the varied entrance of the agents of the donor, the dwarves. This same process will be repeated in the section dealing with Beorn the Skin-changer. They appear on Bilbo's doorstep by degrees, singly or in pairs, but always in increasing permutations of the first entrance: first appears Dwalin; then in like manner Balin; then a pair ("'Kili at your service!' said the one. 'And Fili!' added the other."); followed by threes, Bifur, Bofur, and Bombur; and by fives, Dori, Nori, Ori, Oin, and Gloin—the names provide the clue to this snowballing effect.

The next step in this first division of *Departure* consists of the first "move" in the mythic structure: crossing the first threshold leads the troupe, on the first leg of the journey, into a confrontation with villainy in the person of several trolls. This encounter will serve as prelude to the more serious types of villainy the company must face further along the road of the quest. Here the villainy is of type (A^1), Threat of Cannibalism. Having trapped all the dwarves in nasty-smelling sacks, the trolls cannot decide "whether they should roast them slowly, or mince them fine and boil them, or just sit on them one by one and squash them into jelly." This dispute proves to be their downfall, for Gandalf, hidden in the bushes, keeps the row smoking until the trolls are trapped by the first rays of the sun and turned to stone. An important connective element should be recognized here in that the villainy of the trolls works toward their own destruction instead of finishing off their victims. Villainy defeats its own purposes often enough through its very nature as evil. W. H. Auden raised this point in his essay on the oppositions in *LOTR* when he considered the fact that Sauron was defeated by himself as much as by his adversaries:

> A good person always enjoys one advantage over an evil person, namely, that, while a good person can imagine what it would be like to be evil, an evil person cannot imagine what it would be like to be good. Elrond, Gandalf, Galadriel, Aragorn are able to imagine themselves as Sauron and can therefore resist the temptation to use the Ring themselves, but Sauron cannot imagine that anyone who knows what the Ring can accomplish, his own destruction among other things, will refrain from using it, let alone try to destroy it.

One finds this concept repeated time and again, both as motivational elements and as connectives. A further step in the structural development has occurred here, a fine example of the way in which Tolkien causes the narrative to fold back upon itself, a frequent device in the narrative sequence. A particular transformation has been applied to the function (A), defined by Propp as *assimilation*; that is, two separate functions assume the same morphological meaning, and thus the Villainy (A) also becomes (D) the Donor and (F) Acquisition of a Magical Agent. More precisely, this functional variation insures that the villainy of the trolls, which caused them to be turned to stone, allows the company to discover their cave unmolested and to help themselves to the magical blades hoarded there: the villains have become donors of magical agents; (A^1) is assimilated to (D^3) Conflict with Hostile Donor and (F^1) Discovery of Magical Agent. A final observation at this stage of the linear sequence concerns the connective element already mentioned. As stated before, Gandalf fulfills the function of helper or supernatural aid, and in that role he becomes the connective agent between moves. He shows up at the moment of crisis to save the beleaguered company from Tom, Bert, and William, thus providing the transition from this first villainy to the crossing of the first threshold beyond the well-secured valley of Rivendell.

Reaching the valley of the elves, the company has crossed out of the "lands we know," to use Lord Dunsany's term, and stops at the Last Homely House on the very edge of the Wild, the dwelling of Elrond Half-elven. Once they leave the valley, they will be setting out on the second part of the quest, the *Initiation* or Road of Trials, or in Propp's terms, the Complication, containing seven related moves. Let us very briefly examine these moves of the *Initiation* for folkloristic structure and content. The first villainy that occurs is the capture of the company by goblins in the Misty Mountains. An important connective incident is the escape of Gandalf in the confusion. It has been noted that Gandalf seems to appear out of nowhere in the nick of time to rescue his friends. The reason behind these sudden appearances is quite clear if we use the morphological analysis. Gandalf fulfills the function (B) or Mediation, the connective incident. He provides the bridge from one move to the next. This same technique is employed with greater facility in *LOTR*, not only in the person of Gandalf but by Aragorn as well. As noted, then, Gandalf reappears in the midst of the goblins in time to save his friends and lop off the head of the Great Goblin: "Suddenly a sword flashed in its own light. Bilbo saw it go right through the Great Goblin as he stood dumbfounded in the middle of his rage. He fell dead, and the goblin soldiers fled before the sword shrieking into the darkness." We have in this first move the sequence (A^2) The Attempt to Murder employing a complication of the type $(H\text{-}I)$, Battle With and Defeat of the Villain. The mediation is accomplished, as we said, by the timely return of Gandalf.

The second move is of the same basic sequence (AHI), with the shift from force to a contest of wits (H^2). We are referring to Bilbo's encounter with Gollum and their riddle game in which Bilbo escapes by cleverness rather than battle, (I^2) Superiority in Contest. One should note here that the connective incident occurs in the form of an inverted villainy, that is, Bilbo finds Gollum's magical ring, (A^3) Seizure of a Magical Agent or Helper, followed by $(F$ negative$)$ in which the agent is not transferred to the original owner. The element of finding a magical agent has undergone repetition (recall that the elvish blades having magical power against goblins were found in the troll cave), this time with implications far surpassing the first instance. In fact, we may plumb the motivations even deeper on this point by determining that the function of the connective is really (F^2) The Agent Appears of Its Own Accord; that is, the Ring allows itself to be found by the hobbit, seemingly choosing to pass out of the hands of Gollum. This is the most pivotal event of the Middle-earth mythology, for it not only emphasizes the immanence of power in the natural objects of Middle-earth (the powers inherent in the elves and Sauron flowed into the Ring at its making) but provides the fundamental motivating force for this first tale and the larger one to come. The possession of the Ring gives to the hero the attribute of invisibility, which in the present tale undergoes repetition by appearing in each of the succeeding moves as the means of rescue: from the spiders, the wood-elves, Smaug the dragon, and in the battle of the Three Armies from the dwarves. A final observation of this move discloses that the death of the Great Goblin also becomes a connective function in that it provides the motivation for several of the moves that follow, in particular the concluding move.

The Goblin's demise is motivation for the pursuit by the lesser goblins and wild wargs, ending in the entrapment of the company in trees ringing the foothills of the Misty Mountains. Here a paired set of functions follows the villainy (A^2) Threat of Murder; the functions (H-I) mentioned before appear with the elements (Pr^1) Pursuit of the Hero in an attempt to destroy him and ($Rs1$) Rescue by Air, when the eagles drawn by the yammering and yelping swooped down upon the goblins and "the dark rush of their beating wings smote them to the floor or drove them far away; their talons tore at goblin faces." The connective incident here is (G^1) Transference of Hero to Designated Place, in this case by air, when the eagles deposit the adventurers near the cabin of Beorn, the donor of this same move. The donor follows the form of (D^2) Greeting and Interrogation, to confer his aid, also accompanied by repetition of auxiliary elements; the dwarves are introduced to him in the same manner in which Bilbo encountered them, by degrees and in pairs or name groups, while Gandalf keeps the intimidating shapeshifter's attention distracted with the tale of their ordeal in reaching his settlement (B^2, Announcement of Misfortune): "Mr. Baggins saw then how clever Gandalf had been. The interruptions had really made Beorn more interested in the story, and the story had kept him from sending the dwarves off at once like suspicious beggars. . . . Now he had got fifteen strangers sitting on his porch!"

The connecting functions for the next move occur in the form of (a^1) Lack of a Helper and (A^4) Casting a Spell. The new villainy of the confrontation with the spiders in the forest of Mirkwood is a result of the fact that Gandalf decides to leave the troupe on their own just as they enter the forest, and once in the forest they break his interdiction to stay on the path and avoid the enchantment of the wood-elves. The sequence once again follows the pattern of battle with and victory over the villains, Bilbo again making use of the invisibility granted by the power of the Ring. His cleverness again becomes evident as he leads the spiders off on a wild chase to rescue his friends; from now on the dwarves expect him to figure out what to do as a matter of course; his stature as a hero has begun to develop noticeably. This same gradual development of heroic qualities can also be recognized in the second Ringbearer, Frodo.

The next move includes their capture by the wood-elves, (A^5) Capture and Imprisonment, and the rescue performed as before by Bilbo with the aid of the magic Ring. The type of complication involved here, however, is not (H-I) but rather (M-N) a Difficult Task and its Solution, the task being to discover a method for releasing the dwarves from their elvish prison. This sequence is repeated within the same move when the company find themselves high on the Lonely Mountain trying to uncover the secret entrance mentioned by the map and opened only by the silver key. Again, Bilbo solves the riddle, just in time to make use of the key as "a red ray of the sun escaped like a finger through a rent in the cloud" exposing in a pinpoint of light the long-sought keyhole.

As on previous occasions in which Bilbo has gone prowling about in the dark tunnels under mountains, he provides the connective motivation for the next move by a function of reversed villainy, (A^6) Plundering or Theft; that is, Bilbo lifts a golden cup from under the steaming nose of the great red-gold dragon. This is an excellent example of the growth of heroism in Bilbo, accentuated by Smaug's dream of "a warrior, altogether insignificant in size but provided with a bitter sword and a great courage" troubling his ancient sleep. The actual villainy of this move, however, is the assault of Smaug upon the men of Laketown at the bottom of the foothills, where once again the functions are (H-I). As before, evil engenders its own downfall, for Smaug is killed by the black-shafted arrow of Bard, which pierces the only unprotected spot in the diamond waistcoat of the worm. The dragon's pride in the jewels encrusted on his breast from lying on the hoard for centuries causes him to forget the bare spot over his heart.

As the threads of the narrative pull together, the connectives and motivational functions become more complex, particularly in the crucial move of the *Initiation*, bringing about the climax of the quest. Both functions (a^2) Threat of Murder and (A^7) Declaration of War are assimilated into the beginning of this next move; a lack (Thorin cannot find the Arkenstone because it has been stolen by his own burglar, Tolkien's masterful touch of irony), caused once again by the inverted villainy of the hero perpetrating a theft of a wondrous object, is assimilated with the villainy of a declaration of hostilities. The dwarves are pitted against the elves and men who come to claim part of the treasure as their due for killing the frightful guardian of the hoard. Through the effects of repetition, the war of greed mushrooms into a war of survival when the forces of the mountain goblins pour down upon the besiegers at the same moment as the dwarvish reinforcements of Dain from the Iron Hills reach the site of battle. Aid reappears in the form of the eagles and Beorn. Other connective incidents operative here are the unexpected return of Gandalf among the troops from Laketown and his performance of the function (F neg) in refusing to return the Arkenstone to Thorin. The death of Thorin in battle is the final statement of the self-destructive attribute of evil, for once the dwarvish greed had advanced in Thorin to the point that he was willing to kill and declare war because of it, his hours were numbered.

The victory of the forces of good over the goblins and wargs brings the tale to the *Return*, in which Bilbo and company, laden with gifts from the treasure pile (W^1, Gain of Wealth at Denouement), return to the ordinary daylight world of the "lands we know." This comprises the final move, in which the villainy is of a homely kind, appropriate to its location in Hobbiton: Bilbo's relatives have confiscated his lovely hobbit hole because his year's absence has convinced them he is dead. The function (Q) Recognition of Hero brings about the sequence (H-I^3) Expulsion of the Villain, as he puts an end to the auction being carried out in his front yard. In the three-part scheme of the hero quest, the returning wanderer often finds readmission to society a difficult matter, even though he may have brought back a wonderful boon to the people or profited himself by the venture. As the reader can discern, the sedentary hobbits were now wary of the prodigal: "he was in fact held by all the hobbits of the neighbourhood to be 'queer'"; yet to his credit "he remained an elf-friend, and had the honour of dwarves, wizards, and all such folk as ever passed that way."

The forces of opposition and the pull toward mediation or resolution have been demonstrated on the structural level of the linear sequence, with some slight indication of the same operations at work in the content and mythic motifs that make up the substance of the tale. We find instances of opposition in the delineation of character as well as action. J. S. Ryan's analysis of Tolkien's use of the "literary folk memory" gives the following example: against the winged manifestation of "the dragon symbol as a means of showing opposing evil in the world" Tolkien sets the eagles "as supreme forces of good which appear at decisive moments in both the great battle sequences [of *The Hobbit* and *LOTR*]." Or on a broader level, the use of repetition is also a method for injecting irony into the tale as well as emphasis. The hero returns from peril as the bringer of the grail to humanity. Bilbo the burglar has freed the Lake people from Smaug's tyranny of fear, reestablished Bard as lord in the ruined city of Dale, and brought into the community of Hobbiton fabulous wealth, which he gives away, as well as having helped reinstate the dwarves once more in their old halls under the Lonely Mountain. Yet he also bears into Hobbiton the One Ring, causing the sleepy region of nonadventurous folk to become the seat of the most dread evil and power imaginable, but a power that will also free the world of Middle-earth from the clutches of Sauron once the Ring is destroyed. Thus the local boon for Hobbiton will develop into the universal boon for the wide world. As Lévi-Strauss predicted, there is both logic and continuity in even the most seemingly simple mythic tale.

PAUL H. KOCHER

A Mythology for England

In a paper read at Exeter College, Oxford, in 1912 J. R. R. Tolkien praised the mythological ballads of *Kalevala*, Finland's national epic, as being "full of that very primitive undergrowth that the literature of Europe has on the whole been steadily cutting and reducing for many centuries with different and earlier completeness among different people." And he added, "I would that we had more of it left—something of the same sort that belonged to the English."

In other words, Tolkien, looking about him at extant Anglo-Saxon literature, saw that it had lost much, or most, of its early mythology, as compared with the Norse-Icelandic *Eddas* and sagas and with the *Kalevala*. All that survived were *Beowulf*, the Christian legends of Cynewulf, some historical war poems, one or two minstrel reflections like *Deor's Lament*, letters between husband and wife, miscellaneous charms and riddles, and the like. Not promising materials on which to build a mythology.

Tolkien therefore set out upon the heroic task of remedying this lack by creating "a mythology for England." He wrote in 1914 a poem, "The Voyage of Eärendil, the Evening Star," inspired by Cynewulf's *Crist*. By 1917 he had composed "The Fall of Gondolin" and also "The Children of Húrin," part of which he derived consciously from the story of Kullervo in *Kalevala*.

Writing of this ambition many years later, Tolkien said, "Do not laugh!

From *A Reader's Guide To The Silmarillion* by Paul H. Kocher. © 1980 by Paul H. Kocher.

But once upon a time . . . I had a mind to make a body of more or less connected legend, ranging from the large and cosmogonic to the level of romantic fairy-story—the larger founded on the lesser in contact with the earth, the lesser drawing splendour from the vast backcloths—which I could dedicate simply: to England, to my country. It should possess the tone and quality that I desired, somewhat cool and clear, be redolent of our 'air' (the clime and soil of the North West, meaning Britain and the hither parts of Europe; not Italy or the Aegean, still less the East) and while possessing . . . the fair elusive beauty that some call Celtic (though it is rarely found in genuine ancient Celtic things) it should be 'high,' purged of the gross, and fit for the more adult mind of a land long steeped in poetry. I would draw some of the great tales in fullness and leave many . . . only sketched. The cycles should be linked to a majestic whole, and yet leave scope for other minds and hands, wielding paint and music and drama. Absurd."

In spite of the defensive modesty which led Tolkien to speak of his undertaking as absurd and laughable, he was utterly serious in his design to create a mythology for England. His lifelong labors on it show that. What is important for us to mark well at the outset, in order to understand his purpose, is to see clearly the qualities which Tolkien intended his myths to have and not to have. He wanted them to be "cool and clear . . . redolent of our 'air,'" possessed of "a fair elusive quality," and finally "high, purged of the gross."

He need not have been so critical of his own patriotic wish to provide England with a fitting mythology. The minstrel singing the opening Runo of *Kalevala*, for instance, had no such hesitations. He roundly declared to his Finnish audience that he would sing "the people's legends, / And the ballads of the nation" in order to instruct them, and especially the younger generation, in their heroic past.

Noteworthy in Tolkien's prescription for his new mythology is the number of other mythologies it excludes. It will not resemble Roman and Greek myth. Nor will it borrow from "ancient Celtic things." Since it is to be "high, purged of the gross," it cannot very well look too closely to *Kalevala* either, because Tolkien himself, although enjoying its songs, characterized its heroes as "unhypocritical, low-brow, and scandalous."

Tolkien's prescription for the subject matter of his myths inevitably dictated also the prose style in which he presented them. He was capable of writing in many different styles, of course, but the "cool, clear, high" theme of *The Silmarillion* seemed to him to require a manner which was lofty, and perhaps a little archaic. This style takes some getting used to but, once accepted, its poise can be seen as highly appropriate to its theme. It must be added that some of Tolkien's critics have not accepted it yet, to their own loss.

The mythologies of Rome, Greece, Finland, and the Celtic past having been excluded as models for his new mythology for England, what other mythologies were left to inspire Tolkien and help guide his way? The one which dominated "the hither parts of Europe"—Denmark, Germany, Norway, and especially Iceland—before Christianity came to expunge it, dealt with the Norse pantheon of gods headed by Odin. With this mythology Tolkien was already acquainted as early as 1913, and the more he studied the Icelandic *Elder Edda* (Poetic) and *Younger Edda* (Prose) the more engrossed he became. For them and for the great individual Icelandic sagas, like those that told of Grettir and Njal, he developed a lifelong affection. At the University of Leeds he set up an informal reading club known as the Viking Club, and later at Oxford the Kolbitar, in order to discuss them outside the classes he taught. Indeed *The Silmarillion* resembles *The Elder Edda* in that both are collections of tales more or less loosely tied together, although *The Silmarillion*'s linkage is much tighter and more dramatic, as well as more weighty in meaning.

Account must also be taken of the fact that as a devout Catholic Tolkien rejected much of the world outlook assumed by Norse-Icelandic mythology, although this rejection did not prevent him from admiring the artistic power with which it was often stated, and even accepting into *The Silmarillion* those of its contents most closely akin to Christianity, or those which he could transform into Christian acceptability. No doubt Tolkien told himself, in effect, that the England for which he was inventing a new mythology was officially Christian in his day, that many of his readers would likewise be Christian, and that his proffered mythology ought to be one which could be conceived of as a precursor to that religion, or at least not inimical to it.

One portion of Norse-Icelandic mythology which he cut off cleanly and completely was its polytheistic assembly of some twelve gods (e.g., Odin, Thor, Tyr) and an equal number of goddesses (Frigg, Freya, Var), often their wives. Like the Christian Book of Genesis *The Silmarillion* has, of course, only one God, known as Eru the One or, in his creative aspect, Ilúvatar. It likewise rejects the three Norns or Fates, Urd (Past), Verdandi (Present), and Skuld (Future). These three predetermined the fates not only of men but also of the Norse gods themselves, and nobody could say them nay. Such a doctrine was abhorrent to Tolkien, who believed passionately in free will, as all his writings demonstrate.

As to the origins of the world, Norse-Icelandic mythology taught that it all began with a Void (Ginnunga, gap), "a grinning gap," as it has been strikingly translated. This was likewise the view in the Book of Genesis; so Tolkien had no difficulty in transporting it into *The Silmarillion*. What he could not accept was the Norse belief that the first physical occupant of this emptiness was the frost giant Ymir, said to have been composed of poison drops from some unknown somewhere, perhaps from Elivagur, meaning the Milky Way. The sweat of Ymir's body became nodules which developed into other frost giants. According to *The Elder Edda* there was also a cow (Audhimla), which by licking salty ice blocks uncovered a manlike being named Buri, whose son Bor sired the first gods of the Norse pantheon, Odin, Vili, and Ve. These three then killed Ymir in order to use portions of his body to build Midgard (Middle-earth). Out of his blood they made rivers, lakes, and the sea encircling Midgard; from his flesh, the earth; from his bones, the mountains. Man (Ask) and Woman (Embla) were shaped by Odin and his brothers from two trees they found along the seashore, bestowing on them spirit, understanding, speech, and all the senses proper to humankind. And the three gods used the sparks and burning embers blown out of Muspell to make stars, sun, and moon to light heaven and earth.

For obvious reasons this complex and all too physical account of Creation did not attract Tolkien. And, like the Book of Genesis, *The Silmarillion* puts into the Void only pure Spirit, God the Father (Eru-Ilúvatar) and the angels (Ainur) he has brought into being. For Men, as the second Children of Ilúvatar, Tolkien had plans different from both the Norse and the Biblical narratives, as will be seen.

Like the Norse myth of the world's beginning, the Norse conception of its ending in the Twilight of the Gods (Ragnarök) was quite uncongenial to Tolkien and won no place in *The Silmarillion*. For one thing, Ragnarök had all been predestined by the Norns and could not be prevented even by the gods on Asgard. Indeed all its events were well known to them in advance. The Fenris wolf would devour Odin. Thor and the Midgard Serpent would kill each other. The hosts from fiery Muspellheim led by Surt would come riding to burn the whole of Midgard and cause it to sink under the sea. Wolves would swallow both the sun and the moon. On the plain in Asgard called Vigrid, the Einherjar (those bravest of warriors slain in battle and brought to Valhalla by the Valkyries) would fight in vain to the last man against the invading armies from Muspellheim. Universal anarchy would follow.

This grimmest of prospects threw a shadow over Norse temperament and its whole outlook on life. It had to be endured, however. As Tolkien remarked in his lecture "Beowulf: the Monsters and the Critics," the poem called upon man's heroic will to face the fact that human life is tragic. Norse mythology is full of tales showing Odin wandering about in disguise to gather from the Wise all the information he can get, not to avoid Ragnarök, which he knows cannot be done, but to find out, if he can, when it will come and what, if anything, will happen afterward. That, for example, is the object of Odin's questioning of the Sybil in *The Elder Edda*. In *The Silmarillion* this atmosphere likewise ruled the Noldor exiles in Beleriand, for they had heard the Doom of Mandos, telling them as they left Valinor that they would never win their war against Morgoth. And they knew that Mandos spoke for Ilúvatar. Yet they fought on, their leaders and their cities falling one by one.

There is a kind of happy ending after Ragnarök for the world, for gods, and for men, Sybil tells Odin. True, he and all the other gods must perish in Ragnarök, but their sons will survive to take over their powers. Odin's Vídar and Váli will dwell in Asgard in his stead. Thor's sons Modi and Magni will wield his great hammer Mjöllnir. Moreover, Baldr the beloved will return from the underworld to rule an earth newly risen from the sea. A man and a woman, Lif and Lifthrasir, hidden from Surt in a wood, will be alive to start the human race again. All will be Utopian.

There are hints here and there in *The Silmarillion* that Middle-earth will be destroyed in a Last Battle, but Tolkien prefers not to give even the vaguest details about it or about its aftermath, if any. Specifically, he is too good a Christian himself to bring into his epic another Baldr, or to promote him as some kind of Christ figure. Baldr was a good and just god but he did not voluntarily die on the Cross, or anywhere else, to atone for the sins of the human race as Jesus did.

It is worth mentioning that Loki may have given Tolkien a hint or two for the character of Melkor, before he graduated into full evil as Morgoth. Both are spirits of malice, and both like to perpetrate their plots secretly through others who shield them from all blame. Melkor's method of spreading vile and harmful rumors so subtly that they cannot be traced back to him is well known to readers of *The Silmarillion*. Similarly Loki, having learned that Baldr the beloved is vulnerable only to arrows of mistletoe, does not shoot one at Baldr himself but covertly persuades blind Hödur to do so, killing Baldr. And when Hel, the ruler of the underworld, agrees to release Baldr if every living creature on Midgard will weep for him, Loki assumes a disguise and alone refuses to join in the universal weeping, feeling safe enough behind his change of shape. Finally, at Ragnarök he turns against his fellow gods and guides the fire giants from Muspell to the plain of Vigrid, where the Einherjar are all to be defeated and slain again. So Loki is no mere mischief-maker, as he is sometimes portrayed by some who write about him today, but a full-fledged evildoer, a murderer.

We have read so much about Elves and their mighty deeds in Tolkien's writings that we have come to accept them as possessing always the immortal bodies and splendid minds with which he endowed them. The fact is otherwise. Since at least as far back as Shakespeare's *Midsummer Night's Dream* and Drayton's *Nymphidia* in the sixteenth century, Elves had come to be regarded as tiny, pretty, and fairylike, mere playfellows for young children. Against this conception Tolkien waged incessant war. He did so in his Andrew Lang Lecture "On Fairy-Stories" delivered at the Scottish

University of St. Andrews in 1938. And again at the very end of Appendix E to *The Lord of the Rings* (1955). And yet again in that nostalgic short story, "Smith of Wootton Major" (1967).

Now it happens that Elves are quite prominent in the two *Eddas*, although no detailed physical description of them is given. The Light Elves have a home region (Alfheim), as do the Dark Elves (Svartalfheim). The former seems to lie in Utgard, the outer edge of Earth, the latter underground. "The Light Elves," says *The Prose Edda*, "are fairer than the sun to look upon, but the Dark Elves blacker than pitch."

The Light Elves are friendly with the gods of Asgard. In "Loki's Flyting," when Aegir, god of the sea, gives a feast he invites elves as well as gods and all sit at the same table side by side. In "Skirnir's Ride" the sun is called "Glory of Elves." In the same poem Frey, desiring to possess Gerd, laments, "no elf, no god will grant my prayer," and when Skirnir comes to her, Gerd asks him, "Are you one of the elves, are you one of the gods . . . ?" This close juxtaposition of gods and elves is constant in *The Elder Edda* and indicates that the elves have qualities which are godlike. Examples of this nearness could be multiplied. Finally, we get in "Words of the All-Wise" a list of the names given by Elves to a dozen natural phenomena. These help to reveal the character of elves in Norse mythology.

OBJECTS NAMED	NAMES GIVEN BY ELVES
Earth	Growing
Heaven	Fair-Roof
Moon	Tally-of-Years
Sun	Fair-Wheel
Clouds	Weather-Might
Wind	Traveling-Tumult
Calm	Day-Quiet
Sea	Water-Charm
Fire	All-Burner
Forest	Fair-Bough
Night	Sleep-Pleasure
Seed	Water-Charm

Why the elfin names for Sea and Seed should both be Water-Charm is hard to say, unless it is because Seed also needs water to charm it into growth. The names, on the whole, show imagination, close observation, and a feeling for language.

Consequently it seems more than a mere guess that Tolkien built upon the suggestions of the *Eddas* in reaching his conception of what an Elf truly was, and why he resisted centuries of tradition in formulating it.

The Dwarves of Midgard raise for us the same sort of questions: Whence did they come? What were their true natures? And did they perhaps help Tolkien in conceiving the Dwarves who appear in *The Silmarillion*, *The Hobbit*, and *The Lord of the Rings*?

At the outset be it noted that he had no such long tradition of prettification to combat in the case of the Dwarves as he had in the case of the Elves. At least he nowhere inveighed against it when describing Dwarves. It would seem that in Western folklore and legend Dwarves had always been craftsmen of superlative skill who lived by preference underground or in caves.

According to "The Deluding of Gylfi" Dwarves began as maggots tunneling through the body of Ymir. Hence their propensity for digging down under the surface of Midgard. But by decree of the Aesir gods "they acquired human understanding and the appearance of men, although they lived in the earth and in rocks. Módsognir was the most famous, and next to him, Durin."

At this point *The Elder Edda* tells in "Song of the Sybil" (stanzas 13 ff.) how the gods took counsel as to which of the Dwarves should "mold man by mastercraft / From Ymir's blood and limbs," and chose Durin for the task. Under his direction the Dwarves made "many man-forms . . . from the earth." The names of several dozen Dwarf workmen are then listed. This account of the creation of mankind contradicts the account in *The Prose Edda* that the first man (Ask) and first woman (Embla) were created by the gods out of two trees they found on the seashore. Be that as it may, the tale in *The Elder Edda* establishes the ability of the Dwarf race to plan and execute works of the highest difficulty.

Like the Elves, the Dwarves have dwellings of their own on the outer edge of Midgard, in regions appropriately called Darkdale and Everfrost since the Dwarves prefer darkness and a far northern region where the sun is weak and cold.

Among the chief works forged by their skills are a sword which will never rust and will easily cut through iron ("The Wakening of Angantyr"); a ship, Skidbladnir, which will always have a favorable wind wherever it sails, can hold all the gods, and when not in use can be folded together like a cloth and be kept in a pocket ("The Deluding of Gylfi"); and a mead which makes anyone who drinks it "a poet or a scholar" ("Poetic Diction" in *The Prose Edda*).

Like the Elves, the Dwarves have given names to many natural objects and times ("The Words of the All-Wise"):

Heaven	Dripping-Hall
Moon	The Bright One
Sun	Dvalin's Doll [Dvalin is a Dwarf king]
Calm	Day-Rest

Sea	Dark-Deep
Night	Spinner of Dreams

These namings reveal an imagination and a love of beauty not usually attributed to the dour Naugrim.

Tolkien, however, has always insisted upon their love of beauty. In *The Silmarillion* the Dwarves who build Menegroth of the Thousand Caves for Doriath take the pride of the artist in their work. And in *The Lord of the Rings* Gimli goes into rhapsodies as he examines the sculptures in the caves of Aglarond in Helm's Deep.

Taken all in all, Norse mythology ordains a grim life and a death by fire or by monsters for all the races and the gods of Midgard. In *The Silmarillion* Tolkien, too, has chosen to narrate a series of mistakes and mishaps which are almost uniformly dark, and in which the moments of happiness are few. Not that these errors are predestined, as are those in the *Eddas* and in other early Icelandic lays and sagas. There are no Norns in *The Silmarillion*, only free choices made by free wills. Yet these choices are used by Ilúvatar to help bring about the designs of his Providence. He foreknows them all and fits them into his plans for the future, whatever these may be.

So dismal is the trend of events in *The Silmarillion* "from the high and beautiful to darkness and ruin" that Tolkien appends to its conclusion what is almost an apology, and an extenuation. The woes just related, he declares, were due to the marring of Arda by Morgoth, that is, to the working of Evil in the hearts of Elves and Men, and even in some of the Ainur.

The present chapter contains no mention of Hobbits, the sturdy, brave little Halflings whom many of Tolkien's admirers have taken to their hearts as the best of all his creations. But Hobbits were not to settle in the Shire until the Third Age, thousands of years after the events recounted in *The Silmarillion*. The First Age, of course, deals primarily with Elves, and for them at least as good a case can be made as Tolkien's masterpieces. These potent beings, about whom Norse mythology offered many attractive general hints but few details, became in Tolkien's mind and imagination a wholly new race, the Firstborn Children of Ilúvatar, immortal and wise, superbly worthy to be one of the races for whose sake Eä, an entire world, came into existence. Considering the many ancient misrepresentations of Elves which Tolkien had to overcome, his achievement is amazing. Only less so are his Dwarves, unlike any other race of Dwarves before or since.

But lest Tolkien's skill in creating new races as neighbors for Men absorb all our attention, we should consider also their place in the overall structure he planned for them. How were all the different elements of *The Silmarillion* to be bound together into a coherent whole? "I had a mind," wrote Tolkien to a friend, "to make a body of more or less connected legend, ranging from the large and cosmogonic to the level of romantic fairy-story." And he added that he wanted to "draw some of the great tales in fullness, and leave many only placed in the scheme, and sketched. The cycles should be linked to a majestic whole . . ."

This structure was, in fact, just about what Tolkien achieved. The Music of the Ainur (*Ainulindalë*) and the names and works of the Valar (*Valaquenta*) in the task of creating and serving Eä provide the cosmogony he desired. From it he proceeded to an account of the flight of the Noldor from Valinor and the varying fortunes of their battles against Morgoth (certainly "large," if not "cosmogonic"). And thence to short sketches like the rescue of Maedhros by Fingon and the quest of Aredhel, the White Lady of Noldor. From these to "great tales in fullness," such as the stories of Beren and Lúthien, of Túrin Turambar, and of Tuor's journey to Gondolin.

One can see why Tolkien might not have greatly cared, especially in his old age, about the fact that some episodes of *The Silmarillion* had been fully explored and others only summarized. His design was flexible enough to accommodate every sort of incompleteness save that of a major story left unfinished. There is none such.

When comparing *The Silmarillion* with either *The Elder Edda* or the *Kalevala* we find that these latter two collections start with a Creation and then present a number of tales or lays, in no particular order, about the people created. These tales vary greatly in length and complexity. Tolkien is in the mainstream of mythological writing in all these respects except that as an artist he prefers to give a tighter, more pervasive order to his stories and a more developed theocracy, under Ilúvatar.

NEIL D. ISAACS

On the Need for Writing Tolkien Criticism

The "effort to save Tolkien from the faddists and the button makers," as Rose Zimbardo called our collection first published in 1968, must go on. Indeed, now more than ever, with the publication of a variety of material assembled by Christopher Tolkien under the title *Silmarillion*, the distinctions between the stuff of a cult and the objects of critical literary investigation should be brought sharply into focus.

Tolkien: New Critical Perspectives now appears shortly after the passing of *The Silmarillion* from the best-seller lists following two brief seasons in the sun, but our emphasis remains on *The Lord of the Rings*. We have, after all, a decade's worth of scholarly and critical work to account for, and there is still a general understanding that the trilogy is, if not the heart of Tolkien's work, at least head and shoulders above the rest of his creative corpus. But it is not his only work worthy of attention.

During the decade a rather substantial body of Tolkien criticism has been developed. (We considered offering a comprehensive bibliography here, but since Wayne G. Hammond's addenda to Bonniejean Christensen's list appeared in the *Bulletin of Bibliography* for July–September, 1977, we decided it was unnecessary.) Publication, however, does not tell the whole story. Scarcely a scholarly meeting devoted to twentieth-century literature or science fiction/fantasy/romance or popular culture does not have at least one

From *Tolkien: New Critical Perspectives*, edited by Neil D. Isaacs & Rose A. Zimbardo. © 1981 by The University Press of Kentucky.

paper on Tolkien, and separate MLA seminars have been devoted entirely to him at the national convention.

Perhaps nobody could be expected to keep up with all this activity (though Richard West, in his periodical *Orcrist*, makes a commendable attempt). But it seems to us important to try to distinguish those efforts produced by and for Tolkien *fans* from those which have value for serious students (or readers) of literature. This is a distinction which has not always been made, even by Tolkien's American publishers, who in 1974 issued the enormously simple-minded *Tolkien's World* by Randel Helms just two years after publishing Paul Kocher's excellent *Master of Middle-earth*.

Three collections of essays have made varied contributions to the literature. *The Mankaro Studies in English* volume (1967) contains ten items, of which eight are rather broad discussions that add little to our understanding or appreciation. The exceptions, both by Kathryn Blackmun ("The Development of Runic and Fëanorian Alphabets for the Transliteration of English" and "Translations from the Elvish"), are highly recommended for anyone interested in such matters, but are too specialized to be reprinted here.

Jared Lobdell's *A Tolkien Compass* (1975) is distinguished chiefly by Tolkien's own "Guide to the Names in *The Lord of the Rings*" for the use of translators. The other ten essays may be generally characterized as offering occasional valuable insights, particularly those by Christensen, West, Huttar, and Dorothy Matthews. None seemed so valuable as to demand reprinting here.

Mark Hillegas's *Shadows of Imagination* (1976) had four essays on Tolkien, of which three are worthy of attention: one by Charles Moorman, one by Gunnar Urang, and one by Daniel Hughes. Moorman was represented in our first collection by a chapter from his *Precincts of Felicity*, and we felt that this later essay, which concerns C. S. Lewis as well as Tolkien, would not be appropriate for us. Urang's contribution is a chapter from his *Shadows of Heaven* (Philadelphia, 1971), "Tolkien's Fantasy: The Phenomenology of Hope"; we felt that the positive value of its insights did not justify a second reprinting of an essay that long. As for the original Hughes piece, it is so good that we felt compelled to include it.

Among books on Tolkien that, with the Helms volume, fairly clearly fall into the category of fan fluff are William Ready's *The Tolkien Relation* (1968) and Lin Carter's *Tolkien: A Look behind The Lord of the Rings* (1969). It is difficult to imagine publishers justifying the issue of three comparable books of (loosely defined) literary criticism on any other author or subject than Tolkien. One might reasonably assume that those three were motivated by a common desire to cash in on the cultic phenomena, but the same should not be said for Clyde S. Kilby's *Tolkien and the Silmarillion* (Wheaton, Ill., 1976), though its value is equally slight.

Kilby, who also contributed the fourth Tolkien essay to the Hillegas collection, seems to have had two distinct impulses behind his little book. One is the wish to celebrate his own relationship with Tolkien, for which he can hardly be blamed; perhaps every Tolkien fan will be indulgent on this count. The other is to serve as Tolkien's Christian apologist, describing him as a "staunchly conservative Tridentine Roman Catholic" who had "a special reverence for the Virgin Mary." Kilby asserts, on the basis of "evidence" which he neither cites nor reveals, that Tolkien "intended a final glorious eventuality similar to the one described in the Book of Revelation," and so Kilby as would-be prophet foresaw an end to the "ubiquitous evil of such as Morgoth and Sauron" along with, among other wonders, "the lands lying under the waves lifted up, the Silmarils recovered, Eärendil returned to the earth, the Two Trees rekindled . . . the dead . . . raised and the original purposes of Eru executed."

All this proceeds from the argument that "Tolkien was too pronounced a believer in Christ as the Sovereign Ruler who was to come" not to add all this. Such reasoning takes Kilby's work beyond the bounds of literary criticism. The eschatological glimpses in *The Silmarillion* only serve to put into perspective the proportionally minute use of explicitly Christian mythology in Tolkien's subcreation. This is neither to disparage Kilby's faith nor to discredit Tolkien's, which admittedly could be inferred from the rare clues in the trilogy. The problem is that, while a congenial Christianity may explain some readers' affinity for Tolkien's fiction, a projection of the religion that stands behind the writer provides little illumination of the work itself, and may very often mislead.

There are five books on Tolkien that are worth serious attention by readers. Probably most obvious is Humphrey Carpenter's biography (1977), a thorough, affectionate, but judicious volume. By not presuming to analyze the Tolkien *opera*, Carpenter has provided more insights to the works than he might have had he indulged in detailed critical exegesis. There will no doubt be further biographical attention to Tolkien, but at best Carpenter's book will be joined rather than replaced.

From Australia comes J. S. Ryan's *Tolkien: Cult or Culture?* (Armidale, N.S.W., 1969), an interesting collage, including essays by other hands as separate chapters. Not readily available in this country, the book, despite its title and uneven quality, deserves consideration. We include here a more fully developed version of one of the chapters by Ryan.

The essays by Catharine Stimpson in the Columbia Essays on Modern Writers (1969) and Robley Evans in the *Writers for the 70's* series (1972) may be usefully considered together. Both confront the issue of popular appeal, with quite different results. Stimpson comes down quite solidly against Tolkien, suggesting that unlike Joyce's energy which forged "borrowed elements together to make his work transcendent," Tolkien's "earnest vision seems syncretic, his structure a collage, and his feeling antiquarian." Her dubious implicit definition of "modern" objects to the "many, many echoes" in *The Lord of the Rings*. Evans, on the other hand, seems pleased to discover echoes, assuming that there is a place in the 1970s and beyond for writers who evoke associations with classical, medieval, Renaissance, and romantic traditions, not to mention the popular narrative art of the Victorian period.

Stimpson's "modernist" position leads inevitably to a rejection of Tolkien on political grounds: "Tolkien's stubborn, self-deluding conservatism also demands that we respect families and dynasties. The personal consequence? Chromosomes are destiny. The political consequence? Hereditary power. The social consequence? A rigid class system." Worse, "Tolkien is irritatingly, blandly, traditionally masculine" with an attitude toward sex that is "a little childish, a little nasty, and evasive." Evans, who does not feel called upon to vote for Tolkien, and who may share Stimpson's anticlassist, antisexist, antiageist, antitraditionalist attitudes for all we know, nevertheless finds in *The Lord of the Rings* bases for continued appeal to contemporary audiences.

The trouble with this point counterpoint is rhetorical imbalance. For the purposes of literary judgment, Stimpson operates from a crippling set of political biases. But next to Evans's propriety her one-liners are irresistible. "Tolkien is bogus; bogus, prolix, and sentimental. His popularization of the past is a comic strip for grown-ups. *The Lord of the Rings* is almost as colorful and easy as *Captain Marvel*. That easiness is perhaps the source of Tolkien's appeal. His intellectual, emotional, and imaginative energies are timid and jejune." It is hard to gainsay that Tolkien is "a kindly pediatrician to the soul" and impossible not to smile at "Frodo lives, on borrowed time." For a full and proper response to Stimpson (and other devaluers of Tolkien), the reader should turn to Paul Kocher's *Master of Middle-earth*—or perhaps to *Tolkien: New Critical Perspectives*.

We begin with Lionel Basney's original essay, which treats Tolkien's creation of myth and "feigned history" and incidentally sets aside the cultic distractions of Middle-earth fandom. Next J. S. Ryan deals with critical principles enunciated by Tolkien at a time when he was barely beginning *The Lord of the Rings* and shows that he practiced what he preached. Ryan uses the short story "Leaf by Niggle" as his example, "an allegory of . . . the artist's creative exercise."

The next three essays relate Tolkien's material in *The Lord of the Rings* to a variety of traditions. Verlyn Flieger's contribution, adapted from her 1977 Catholic University dissertation, urges the value of recognizing the medieval heritage of Tolkien's heroes. Rose Zimbardo's focus is on the structure of the trilogy which she relates to the Renaissance concept of *discordia concors*. Then Daniel Hughes extends the frame of reference for Tolkien's readers to the high romantic tradition of Coleridge, Shelley, Wordsworth, Hopkins, Scott, and Blake.

The essay by Patrick Grant, reprinted from *Cross Currents*, moves from Blake's vision and the postromantic tradition of Tolkien and his friends to a careful analysis of *The Lord of the Rings* in terms of Jungian archetypes. In his analysis Grant comes to terms with the Christianity implicit in Tolkien's work in a way that Kilby could not. Then David Jeffrey's original piece moves through considerations of allegory, allusion, and pattern (again with an implicit Christianity) to philological and onomastic concerns. The reader will find examples both challenging and provocative. We next offer the first chapter of Kocher's book, a clear exposition of how Tolkien's created world can be at the same time "a world elsewhere" (as Richard Poirier uses the phrase) and a very real part of our own.

Succeeding essays treat neglected aspects of Tolkien's work. Henry Parks deals with the significance of Tolkien's criticism, not as a guide to reading his fiction, but in its own right as occupying a central position in contemporary critical thought (inevitably this means *vis-à-vis* Northrop Frye); and Lois Kuznets examines *The Hobbit* as a work in the mainstream of traditional British children's literature.

Finally, we offer contrasting reviews of *The Silmarillion*, both well argued and each representative of one of the two dominant critical responses the work has evoked. To Joseph McLellan, its best parts stand up well under comparisons with Hesiod, *The Iliad*, *Paradise Lost*, and Genesis, while to Robert M. Adams it is an "empty and pompous bore." Perhaps both are right. The real paradox is that those who are most eagerly drawn to the book as a major object of their cultic attention will most easily be put off by its remoteness from *The Lord of the Rings*.

It was our considered decision not to wait for full and careful critical analysis of *The Silmarillion* before offering this collection, for several reasons. First, Christopher Tolkien promises at least another volume of material assembled from the fragments of his father's subcreated world, and we think that it should all be judged together. We also think that no individual segment is so significant by itself as to hold up publication, although the metaphor of creation-by-music and the tale of Túrin Turambar (among other attractive items) might well elicit valuable exegesis. Finally, we are ever more firmly convinced that *The Lord of the Rings* is the creative work most worthy of critical attention, and the emphasis of our book reflects that conviction.

The publication of *The Silmarillion* should nevertheless stimulate some reexamination of certain critical issues regarding the trilogy. For example, the question of the appropriateness of the appendixes at the end of *The Return of the King* will have to be reopened. If they are considered integral parts of the esthetic design of *The Lord of the Rings*, could not much of the assembled lore in *The Silmarillion* also be included? Or perhaps all the cosmogonical, cosmological, and apocalyptic material that stands behind the great narrative of the trilogy should be considered to subsume all the back matter—genealogical, philological, onomastic, and gazetteerical—in both books.

Certainly a reexamination of Tolkien's style is in order. As I said in reviewing *The Silmarillion* for the *Washington Star*, its style "will stun many, particularly those who know Tolkien as the author of 'Beowulf: the Monsters and the Critics,' still the most lucid and readable essay in all Old English scholarship. This book is persistently Biblical. The Book of Numbers comes most often to mind. And so it is that, beyond all hope, Christopher son of J. R. R. has brought the new Tolkien to light in the world of men." The point is that new attention will be drawn by contrast to those stylistic aspects of the trilogy that breathe life into its subcreation: narrative power, droll charm, intricate playfulness, and physical and psychological detail. All this is substantially absent from the solemnly sacred text of *The Silmarillion*.

We have had to make some difficult decisions in keeping this book to its present size. Basically, we have been guided by a criterion of broad applicability, so that some very good but comparatively narrow papers were omitted. I think particularly of Veronica Kennedy's folkloristic insights and J. Russell Rearers' "Gandalf as a Bodhissatva." Both, I trust, will be published, as the necessary process of critical elucidation of a major work of art goes on.

T. A. SHIPPEY

Lit. and Lang.

Old Antipathies

'This is not a work that many adults will read right through more than once.' With these words the anonymous reviewer for the *Times Literary Supplement* (25 November 1955) summed up his judgement of J. R. R. Tolkien's *The Lord of the Rings*. It must have seemed a pretty safe prophecy at the time, for of course very few adults (or children) read anything right through more than once, still less anything as long as *The Lord of the Rings*. However it could not have been more wrong. This did not stop critics continuing to say the same thing. Six years later, after the three separate volumes had gone through eight or nine hardback impressions each, Philip Toynbee in the *Observer* (6 August 1961) voiced delight at the way sales, he thought, were dropping. Most of Professor Tolkien's more ardent supporters, he declared, were beginning to 'sell out their shares' in him, so that 'today these books have passed into a merciful oblivion.' Five years afterwards the authorised American paperback edition of *The Lord of the Rings* was moving rapidly past its first million copies, starting a wave which has never receded even to the more-than-respectable levels of 1961.

The point is not that reviewers make mistakes (something which happens too often to deserve comment). It is that they should insist so perversely in making statements not about literary merit, where their

From *The Road to Middle-Earth* by T. A. Shippey. © 1982 by T. A. Shippey.

opinions could rest undisprovable, but about popular appeal, where they can be shown up beyond all possibility of doubt. Matters are not much better with those critics who have been able to bring themselves to recognise the fact that some people do like Tolkien. Why was this 'balderdash' so popular, Edmund Wilson asked himself, in *The Nation* (14 April 1956). Well, he concluded, it was because 'certain people—especially, perhaps, in Britain— have a life-long appetite for juvenile trash.' Some twenty-five years before the same critic had delivered a little homily on the subject of intolerant responses to new fictions, in his book *Axel's Castle:*

> it is well to remember the mysteriousness of the states with which we respond to the stimulus of works of literature and the primarily suggestive character of the language in which these works are written, on any occasion when we may be tempted to characterise as 'nonsense,' 'balderdash' or 'gibberish' some new and outlandish-looking piece of writing to which we do not happen to respond. If other persons say they do respond, and derive from doing so pleasure or profit, we must take them at their word.

A good rule, one must admit! But Mr Wilson had evidently forgotten it by the time he came to read *The Lord of the Rings*: or perhaps every time he said 'we' in the passage just quoted, he really meant 'you.'

Very similar play is made with pronouns in C. N. Manlove's *Modern Fantasy* (1975), a book dedicated to the thesis that no work of modern fantasy has remained 'true to its original vision,' but one which like Edmund Wilson's review does at least confront the problem of Tolkienian popularity—of course much more evident in 1975 than 1956. Dr Manlove also thinks that the whole thing might be mere national aberration, though he prefers to blame the United States and 'the perennial American longing for roots.' Or could it all be due to mere length?

> Doubtless there is such a thing as the sheer number of pages the reader has had to turn that can add poignancy to the story— one almost feels this is the case as we come to the great close of Malory's epic. But not with Tolkien's book, for we have never been very much involved anyway.

Who are 'we'? Readers of *Modern Fantasy*? Readers of *The Lord of the Rings*? There is no sensible answer to the question. For all the display of scholarly reflection this is, just like the bits from Messrs Toynbee and Wilson and the *TLS* reviewer, once more the criticism of blank denial. People won't like *The*

Lord of the Rings, they don't like *The Lord of the Rings*, they've stopped liking *The Lord of the Rings*. Matter closed.

In an exasperated kind of way Tolkien would, I think, have been particularly delighted to read Dr Manlove's essay. He had run into criticism like that before, indeed it is a major theme of his tauntingly-titled British Academy lecture of 1936, '*Beowulf*: the Monsters and the Critics.' The critics he had in mind were critics of *Beowulf*, but they were saying pretty much the same thing: *Beowulf* didn't work, it was intrinsically silly, and 'we' weren't involved with it. 'Correct and sober taste,' Tolkien wrote, 'may refuse to admit that there can be an interest for us—the proud we that includes all intelligent living people—in ogres and dragons; we then perceive its puzzlement in face of the odd fact that it has derived great pleasure from a poem that is actually about these unfashionable creatures.' Tolkien had not, in 1936, realised how quickly 'correct and sober taste' could stamp 'puzzlement' out, and 'pleasure' along with it. However, for the rest he might just as well have been writing about responses to *The Lord of the Rings*. No doubt he would have felt honoured, in a way, to find himself as well as the *Beowulf*-poet driving critics to take refuge in threadbare and hopeless 'we's.'

The similarities between responses to *Beowulf* (as analysed by Tolkien) and to *The Lord of the Rings* do not end there. If one looks at Tolkien's remarks about the *Beowulf* critics, one can see that the thing he found worst about them was their monoglottery: they seemed able to read only one language, and even if they knew a bit of French or some other modern tongue they were quite incapable of reading ancient texts, ancient English texts, with anything like the degree of detailed verbal insight that was required. They relied on translations and summaries, they did not pay close attention to particular words. 'This is an age of potted criticism and pre-digested literary opinion,' Tolkien wrote in 1940 in apologetic Preface to a translation of *Beowulf* which he hoped would only be used as a crib; 'in the making of these cheap substitutes for food translations unfortunately are too often used.' Now this could hardly be said about *The Lord of the Rings*, which is after all mostly in modern English. Or could it? Were people really paying close attention to words, Tolkien must have wondered as he read through the reviews? Or were they just skipping through for the plot again?

His irritation surfaced in the 1966 Foreword to the second edition of *The Lord of the Rings*, where he wrote, rather cattily:

> Some who have read the book, or at any rate have reviewed it, have found it boring, absurd, or contemptible; and I have no cause to complain, since I have similar opinions of their works, or of the kinds of writing that they evidently prefer.

Probably this was, strictly speaking, unfair. All the reviewers I have come across do seem to have read the book right through with no more than a normal run of first-reading miscomprehensions. However it is a surprising fact that Edmund Wilson, who declared that he had not only read the book but had read the whole thousand pages out loud to his seven-year-old daughter, nevertheless managed consistently to spell the name of a central character wrong: 'Gandalph,' for 'Gandalf.' Edwin Muir in the *Observer* preferred 'Gandolf.' This may seem purely trivial; but Tolkien would not have looked at it that way. He knew that 'ph' for 'f' was a learned spelling, introduced sporadically into English from Latin from about the fourteenth century, mostly in words of Greek origin like 'physics' or 'philosophy.' It is not used for native words like 'foot' or 'fire.' Now in the rather similar linguistic correspondences of Middle-earth (they are laid out in Appendices E and F of *The Lord of the Rings*, for those who haven't already noticed) it is clear that 'Gandalf' belongs to the latter set rather than the former. 'Gandalph' would accordingly have seemed to Tolkien as intrinsically ludicrous as 'phat' or 'phool,' or come to that 'elph' or 'dwarph.' He could hardly have conceived of the state of mind that would regard such variations as meaningless, or beneath notice. As for 'Gandolf,' that is an Italian miscomprehension, familiar from Browning's poem 'The Bishop Orders His Tomb,' but wildly inappropriate to a work which does its best to avoid Latinisms.

No compromise is possible between what one might call 'the Gandalph-mentality' and Tolkien's. Perhaps this is why *The Lord of the Rings* (and to a lesser extent Tolkien's other writings as well) makes so many literary critics avert their eyes, get names wrong, write about things that aren't there and miss the most obvious points of success. Tolkien thought this instinctive antipathy was an ancient one: people who couldn't stand his books hadn't been able to bear *Beowulf*, or *Pearl*, or Chaucer, or *Sir Gawain*, or *Sir Orfeo* either. For millennia they had been trying to impose their views on a recalcitrant succession of authors, who had fortunately taken no notice. In the rather steely Preface to their edition of *Sir Gawain and the Green Knight* (in which the word 'criticism' is conspicuously shunned), Tolkien and his colleague E. V. Gordon declared that they wanted to help people read the poem 'with an appreciation as far as possible of the sort which its author may be supposed to have desired.' Doing the same job for Tolkien ought to be easier, since he is so much more our contemporary than the Gawain-poet; on the other hand Tolkien's mind was one of unmatchable subtlety, not without a streak of deliberate guile. However nothing is to be gained by applying to it the criteria of 'correct and sober taste,' of the great but one-sided traditions of later English literature, of those 'higher literary aspirations' so haughtily opposed by Anthony Burgess to 'allegories with animals or fairies' (*Observer*, 26 November 1978). These lead only to the conclusion that there is nothing to be said and no phenomenon to consider. Still, something made Tolkien different, gave him the power so markedly to provoke these twin reactions of popular appeal and critical rage.

The Nature of Philology

Whatever it was, it almost self-evidently had something to do with his job. For most of his active life Tolkien taught Old English, Middle English, the history of the English language; in doing so he was competing with teachers of English literature for time, funds and students, on the whole a thankless task since for all that Tolkien could do the current was setting firmly away from him and from his subjects. Tolkien was by all accounts as capable of keeping up a grudge as the next man, and his minor writings often show it. The anthology of *Songs for the Philologists* which he and E. V. Gordon compiled and had privately printed in 1936 contains at least two poems by Tolkien attacking teachers of 'Lit.'; one of them, titled variously 'Two Little Schemes' and 'Lit. and Lang.,' the worst he ever wrote; so bad indeed that it makes me think (or hope) that something must have gone wrong with it *en route* between poet and printer. Meanwhile he was from the start of his learned career barely able to use the word 'literature' at all without putting inverted commas round it to show he couldn't take it seriously. Thus his famous article on '*Ancrene Wisse* and *Hali Meiðhad*,' published in 1929, opens with the remark that: 'The *Ancrene Wisse* has already developed a "literature," and it is very possible that nothing I can say about it will be either new or illuminating to the industrious or leisured that have kept up with it. I have not.' There are variants on the same innuendo at the start of the *Beowulf* lecture of 1936 and in the *Sir Gawain* Preface of 1925. Of course there is a reason (of characteristic deviousness) for this repeated Tolkienian joke, and one which can easily be extracted from the pages of the *Oxford English Dictionary*, on which Tolkien had himself worked in youth. There one can find that the meaning which Tolkien foisted on to 'literature' is indeed recognised, under heading 3b: 'The body of books and writings that treat of a particular subject.' But why should Tolkien insist on using *that* one when heading 3a is less narrow and much more generally pertinent: 'Literature' meaning 'literary productions as a whole . . . Now also, in a more restricted sense, applied to writing which has claim to consideration on the ground of beauty of form or emotional effect'? The sting for Tolkien lay in the illustrative quotations which form the backbone of the definition, of which the sixth reads 'The full glory of the new literature broke in England with

Edmund Spenser,' i.e. in 1579. The true mordancy of that opinion may not appear till later. It is enough to note that if you took the *OED* seriously you could argue (a) that the valueless accumulation of books about *Beowulf* and the *Ancrene Wisse* and *Sir Gawain* were all 'literature,' under heading 3b, but (b) the original and creative works themselves, all very much pre-1579, were not, under 3a. Naturally no one would be stupid enough to put forward such a proposition seriously and in so many words. Still, Tolkien did not think these semantic tangles entirely fortuitous; the *OED* might not mirror truth but it did represent orthodox learned opinion. It was typical of him to note the confusion and the slur it implied, to use the one to avenge the other—'literature' was 'books about books,' the dead Latin 'letter' opposed to the ancient English spirit.

Yet what this obsessive playing with words shows, better than anything, is that beneath the fog and fury of academic politics, Tolkien realised that all discussions of 'language' and 'literature' were irretrievably poisoned by the very terms they were bound to use. When he was not simply playing for his side, he accepted that 'lang.' was just as foolish a rallying-cry as 'lit.' In his manifesto of 1930, 'The Oxford English School,' he even suggested that both terms should be scrapped in favour of 'A' and 'B.' The same article makes it clear that he thought both 'linguistic' and 'literary' approaches too narrow for a full response to works of art, especially early works of art, and that furthermore what was needed was not some tame compromise between them (which is all most Schools of English usually manage to provide), but something as it were at right angles to both. This third dimension was the 'philological' one: it was from this that he trained himself to see things, from this too that he wrote his works of fiction. 'Philology' is indeed the only proper guide to a view of Middle-earth 'of the sort which its author may be supposed to have desired.' It is not Tolkien's fault that over the last hundred years 'philology,' as a term and as a discipline, has been getting itself into even worse tangles than 'English literature.'

Dictionary definitions are, symptomatically, unhelpful. The *OED*, though conceived and created by philologists and borne along by the subject's nineteenth-century prestige, has almost nothing useful to offer. 'Philology,' it suggests, is: '1. Love of learning and literature; the study of literature in a wide sense, including grammar, literary criticism and interpretation . . . polite learning. Now rare in general sense.' Under 2 it offers 'love of talk, speech or argument' (this is an offensive sense in which philology is mere logic-chopping, the opposite of true philosophy); while 3 recovers any ground abandoned in 1 by saying it is 'The study of the structure and development of language; the science of language; linguistics. (Really one branch of sense 1.)' So 'philology' is 'lang.' and 'lit.' too, all very charitable but too vague to be any use. The *Deutsches Wörterbuch* set in motion by Jacob Grimm (himself perhaps the greatest of all philologists and responsible in true philological style for both 'Grimm's Law of Consonants' and *Grimms' Fairy Tales*) could do little better, defining *philologie* with similar inclusiveness as 'the learned study of the (especially Classical) languages and literatures.' The illustrative quotation from Grimm's own work is more interesting in its declaration that 'none among all the sciences is prouder, nobler, more disputatious than philology, or less merciful to error'; this at least indicates the expectations the study had aroused. Still, if you didn't know what 'philology' was already, the Grimm definition would not enlighten you.

The matter is not cleared up by Holger Pedersen's assertion of 1924 that philology is 'a study whose task is the interpretation of the literary monuments in which the spiritual life of a given period has found expression' (for this leaves you wondering why 'spiritual' has been put in and 'language' for once left out); nor by Leonard Bloomfield's aside a year later, when, proposing the foundation of a Linguistic Society for America, he explicitly rejected the term 'philological' and noted that while British scholars tended to use it to mean 'linguistic,' Americans would prefer to keep the latter term and to revere philology rather more from a distance as 'that noblest of sciences . . . the study of national culture . . . something much greater than a misfit combination of language plus literature.' Anyway some Britons were very far removed from his position. John Churton Collins, nineteenth-century man of letters and candidate for an Oxford Chair, had written in 1891 (it was part of his campaign to keep men like Joseph Wright, Tolkien's tutor, *out* of any prospective English School at Oxford):

> it [i.e. philology] too often induces or confirms that peculiar woodenness and opacity, that singular coarseness of feeling and purblindness of moral and intellectual vision, which has in all ages been the characteristic of mere philologists . . . [it] too often resembles that rustic who, after listening for several hours to Cicero's most brilliant conversation, noticed nothing and remembered nothing but the wart on the great orator's nose.

Opinions such as this clung on a long time in England. Tolkien wrote in 1924 '"Philology" is in some quarters treated as though it were one of the things that the late war was fought to end.' When I first read this I took it to be a joke. However just three years before the British Board of Education had printed a Report on *The Teaching of English in England* which declared, among much else, that philology ought not to be taught to undergraduates, that it was a 'German-made' science, and (this comes in a footnote on p. 286) that by contributing to German arrogance it had led in a direct way to the outbreak of World War I.

Philology was 'the noblest of sciences'; it was literary; it was linguistic; it was German; it was Classical; it was different in America; it was about warts on noses; it was 'the special burden of the Northern tongues' (Tolkien speaking); also 'the special advantage they possess as a discipline' (Tolkien once again). This begins to sound like the Babel of conflicting voices which Tolkien guyed so fiercely in his lecture on *Beowulf*, except that in this case the final universal chorus of all voices 'it is worth studying!' would clearly be somewhat ragged. If no single answer to the question 'what is philology?' can be found, at least few authorities would dissent from the view that the redefinition of philology—the moment when it stopped being used in the *OED*'s vaguest senses of 'love of talk' or 'love of learning'—came in 1786 when Sir William Jones informed the Bengal Society in Calcutta that Sanskrit resembled Greek and Latin too strongly for this to be the result of chance, but that all three, together with Germanic and Celtic, must have 'sprung from some common source which, perhaps, no longer exists.'

Obviously this thought must have crossed many minds before 1786, for even between English and Latin, say, there are enough similarities—one, two, three, *unus*, *duo*, *tres*—to make one think there may be some sort of a connection. But until the turn of the eighteenth century such speculations had foundered immediately on the great reefs of dissimilarity surrounding the occasional identical rocks. After all the main thing anyone knew about languages was that they were so different they had to be learnt one at a time. The great alteration Jones and his successors brought to the problem was the idea of looking not for chance resemblances—which had already been used to 'prove' relationships all over the map—but for regular change. *Bad* in modern Persian had the same sound and sense as 'bad' in English (remarked A. E. Pott in 1833), but that was just coincidence. On the other hand *xvāhar* in Persian was originally the same word as *xo* in Ossetic, and both were related to English 'sister'; furthermore the intermediate stages could be inferred and on occasion recovered. Like many mental revolutions, this linguistic one depended on being counter-intuitive. It was also to an intense degree *comparative*, using many languages to explain and corroborate each other; and, since different stages of the same language could be used comparatively, by nature overwhelmingly historical. 'Philology unfolds the genesis of those laws of speech which grammar contemplates as a finished result,' says a citation in the *OED*, dated 1852. Its author did not mean 'philology' in any of the senses quoted from the *OED* on p. 6 above; he meant *comparative* philology, the science inspired by Sir William and carried on through many inheritors to Professor Tolkien himself. One may remark that the confidence with which 'genesis' is approached was characteristic of the time.

By 1852, indeed, 'the new philology' had many triumphs to look back on, with several yet to come: one might pick out the prize-winning essay of Rasmus Rask in 1814, on Old Icelandic, and on the relationship of Scandinavian languages to Slavic, Celtic, Finnish and Classical ones; the enormous 'Comparative Grammar' or *Vergleichende Grammatik* of Franz Bopp in 1833–49, which covered Sanskrit, Zend, Armenian, Greek, Latin, Lithuanian, Old Slavic, Gothic and German; the *Deutsche Grammatik* (1819) of Jacob Grimm, and all their many successors. The point which all these works brandished was the intensely systematic nature of discovery, expressed as time went on increasingly by the word 'laws' (see *OED* citation above), and on the analogy of physics or chemistry by the association of laws with discoverers: Grimm's Law, Verner's Law, Kuhn's Laws Thomsen's Law, etc. There was and still is something insidiously fascinating about the relationships these laws uncover, in such detail and such profusion. Latin *pisces* is the same word as Old English *fisc*, observed Jacob Grimm, or indeed modern English 'fish'; *pes* is the same as 'foot' and *pellis* as 'fell' (the old word for 'skin'). What about *porcus* and 'pig,' though, where the p/f alternation breaks down? Well, there is an Old English word *fearh* which corresponds properly, noted Grimm, its modern descendant being 'farrow,' again an old or dialectal word for a 'birth' of piglets. The mill of comparisons will not work on basic or standard or literary languages alone, but demands ever-increasing grist from older or localised or sub-standard forms. The reward it offers is first an increasing sense that everything can be worked out, given time and material, second an exciting tension between the modern meanings of words—words everyone has known all their lives—and what appear as the ancient meanings. 'Daughter' in modern Hindustani comes out as *beti*; yet there is a connection between the two languages in the word *dudh*, 'milk.' In ancient days, it seems, a word like Sanskrit *duhitar* meant 'the little milker'; but the job was so often given to daughters that task and relationship became fused. It 'opens before our eyes a little idyll of the poetical and pastoral life of the early Aryans,' enthused Max Müller, whose lectures on comparative philology bowled over not only (or not even) the learned world in the 1860s and after, but also London's high society. Comparison was the rage: it didn't tell you only about words, it told you about people.

But somewhere towards the end of the nineteenth century things had begun to go wrong. As is obvious from all that Tolkien ever said about literature and about philology, he felt that he had taken over (perhaps unfairly, but possibly not) a losing position in the academic game from his predecessors. Why—he could hardly have helped wondering—was that? Why had philology so ignominiously belied its promise?

Probably the short answer is that the essence of comparative philology was slog. There is something wistful in Tolkien's astonished praise of the 'dull stodges' of Leeds University, in his insistence that at Leeds anyway 'Philology is making headway . . . and there is no trace of the press-gang!' For matters were different elsewhere. No science, Jacob Grimm had said of philology, was 'prouder, nobler, more disputatious, or *less merciful to error*' (my italics). All its practitioners accepted, to a degree now incredible, a philosophy of rigid accuracy, total coverage, utter right and utter wrong: in 1919 the old and massively distinguished Eduard Sievers happily put his reputation on the line when he offered to dissect a text provided unseen by Hans Lietzmann, and to show from linguistic evidence how many authors had composed it (he had already done the same thing to the Epistles of Paul). He got Lietzmann's specimen totally wrong. But no one said the idea of the test itself was unfair? Further down the scale, the discoveries of Grimm and his successors as far as Ferdinand de Saussure (now famous for inventing 'structuralism' but before that a student of *Ablaut*) were communicated increasingly to students as facts, systems of facts, systems divorced from the texts they had been found in. We must have philology within English Studies, wrote F. York Powell the Icelandicist in 1887, 'or goodbye to accuracy.' The claim was false—you can be accurate about other things besides sound-shifts—but after seventy years of unbroken progress for the subject it was also damningly unambitious. Looking back many years later, R. W. Chambers (the man who turned down the Chair of Anglo-Saxon which eventually went to Tolkien in 1925) summed up success and failure by observing that in 1828 'the comparative philologist was like Ulysses,' but 'Scoffers may say that my parallel is all too true—that students of comparative language, like [Dante's] Ulysses, found only the mountain of Purgatory— Grimm's Law, Verner's Law, Grassmann's Law—rising in successive terraces of horror—and then were overwhelmed . . .' Scoffers said exactly that; their viewpoint became dominant; comparative philology seen as 'hypothetical sound-shiftings in the primeval German forests' went into a decline nearly as precipitate as its rise.

This is why 'philology' has first the old vague sense of 'love of learning'; then the new nineteenth century one of 'study of texts leading to comparative study of language leading to comprehension of its evolution'; and in the twentieth century the specialised meaning, within departments of English Studies, of 'anti-literary science kept up by pedants (like Professor Tolkien) which ought to be stopped as soon as possible.' But these interesting semantic changes leave something out: the 'spiritual life' waved at by Holger

Pedersen, the 'national culture' saluted by Leonard Bloomfield—or, to put it another way, the *Grimms' Fairy Tales*.

Lost Romances

For philology, after the Rask-Bopp-Grimm breakthrough, had moved in other directions beside the phonological and morphological. The mill of historical comparison called increasingly for fresh material, and one natural effect, besides the study of language in general, was the study of languages in particular. Scholars became much more interested in unread texts; they also became spectacularly better at reading them, at producing dictionaries of stone-dead languages. As Tolkien noted himself, the word *hós(e)* in *Beowulf* was never found anywhere else in Old English, so that one would have to guess at its meaning from context, were it not for the fact that philology proved it was the 'same' word as Old High German *hansa*, as in 'Hanseatic League,' with the meaning 'retinue,' or possibly 'band of people connected by mutual oaths.' The dead languages furnished comparative material; the comparative material illuminated dead languages. Men learnt to read Hittite, recognised as an Indo-European language in the 1920s (with marked effect on Old Testament studies), Tokharian (another Indo-European language once spoken by steppe-nomads but now represented mostly by texts preserved accidentally in an oasis in Turkestan), more recently to decipher 'Linear B' (an exploration of Cretan archaeology which would have been impossible in a pre-Bopp era). Much obscurer discoveries were made. A whole nation was theorised to lie behind the tiny fragment of Kottish, a language spoken when it was investigated by only five people. Holger Pedersen said of their relatives the Yenisei that they seem to be 'the last remnants of a powerful folk who, with the Thibetan empire as their southern neighbour, ruled over a great part of Siberia, but were at length compelled to submit to the Turks.' Yet of their rule no traces remain other than linguistic ones. The romance of these investigations can still be felt. It is a large-scale analogue of Müller's remarks on *duhitar*, of the awareness that some forms even of modern language took you back to the Stone Age (as in English 'hammer,' cognate with Old Slavic *kamy*, 'stone'). The romance became stronger, perversely, the closer it got to home.

Thus Old English itself looked very strikingly different after the philologists got hold of it—and it was they who insisted on calling it Old English instead of Anglo-Saxon to mark what they saw as an essential continuity. The story of Gothic, however, was even more dramatic. Some awareness of this language had been around from an early period. People knew that such texts as the Uppsala *Codex Argenteus* were *in* Gothic, that the

Goths were an East Germanic tribe who had overrun parts of the Roman
Empire from about AD 376, that they had been converted to literacy and
Christianity, and become linguistically extinct some time round the eighth
century. Philology shattered this picture. For one thing Gothic became
suddenly more than comprehensible, it became vital: it was the earliest
Germanic language recorded, Germanic was the area of most philologists'
main interest (they were mostly Germans), and Gothic exhibited, in ways
that Old English and Old High German did not, stages in the history of all
the Germanic languages inferable from but not recorded in its cousins. So,
modern English says 'old' but 'elder,' Old English (in its Early West Saxon
form) *eald* but *ieldra*, both say (more or less) 'to heal' but 'hale (and hearty).'
For these Gothic offers respectively *altheis*, *althiza*, *háiljan*, *háils*. The
common element deduced is that when an *-i-* or *-j-* followed *a* or *ái* in *old* Old
English (this goes back to the time before Englishmen had learnt to write)
speakers began to change the earlier vowel into *e*, *æ*—with similar changes
affecting other vowels. Where there is a succeeding *-i-* in Gothic there is a
change of vowel in Old (and often still in modern) English; not otherwise.

   This phenomenon, known as 'i-mutation,' became one of the most
familiar horrors of university philology, but there is in it something both
mysterious and satisfactory: a whole series of things which people said, and
still *say*, without in the least knowing why, turn out to have one very old but
dear, 100 per cent predictable reason. It is almost like genetics. No wonder
that Grimm said Gothic was a 'perfect' language, Tolkien that it took him by
storm. A further stage in the developing romance of 'Gothia' was the
thought that the Goths might *not* be extinct. At some time in the 1560s one
Ogier van Busbecq, a Fleming then acting as ambassador in Istanbul, had
heard some foreigners whose speech sounded familiar. He recorded a list of
words from them and printed it in 1589. They proved to be Gothic, nearly a
thousand years out of place. Their interest aroused several centuries later,
scholars could for a while entertain the hope that a living Gothic was still
somewhere in existence, as a kind of Abominable Snowman of language.
Alas, it wasn't. But at least it became clearer how Gothic had survived, in the
remote Crimea, and it became possible to piece together once again the
history of a vanished people.

   It is not too much to say that this language and this people haunted
Tolkien all his life. As is noted by Christopher Tolkien, the names of the
leaders of the Rohirrim before the dynasty of Eorl are not Old English, like
everything else in the Riders' culture, but Gothic, e.g. Vidugavia, Vidumavi,
Marhwini, etc. They function there to suggest language behind language and
age behind age, a phenomenon philologists so often detected. On a larger
scale the Battle of the Pelennor Fields closely follows the account, in

Jordanes' *Gothic History*, of the Battle of the Catalaunian Plains, in which also the civilisation of the West was preserved from the 'Easterlings,' and in which the Gothic king Theodorid was trampled by his own victorious cavalry with much the same mixture of grief and glory as Tolkien's Théoden. Perhaps the most revealing remark, however, comes in a letter from Tolkien to his son Christopher after the latter had read a paper on the heroes of northern legend. In this he praised his son's paper for the light it shed on men and on history, but added:

> All the same, I suddenly realized that I am a *pure* philologist. I like history, and am moved by it, but its finest moments for me are those in which it throws light on words and names! Several people (and I agree) spoke to me of the art with which you made the beady-eyed Attila on his couch almost vividly present. Yet oddly, I find the thing that thrills my nerves is the one you mentioned casually: *atta, attila*. Without those syllables the whole great drama both of history and legend loses savour for me.

The point is that Attila, though a Hun, an enemy of the Goths under Theodorid, and a byword for bloody ferocity, nevertheless does not appear to bear a barbarian name. 'Attila' is the diminutive form of the Gothic word for 'father,' *atta*: it means 'little father,' or even 'dad,' and it suggests very strongly the presence of many Goths in Attila's conquering armies who found loot and success much more attractive than any questions of saving the West, Rome or civilisation! As with *duhitar*, 'little milker,' or *kamy* as a cognate for 'hammer,' the word tells the story. Tolkien went on in his letter to say that in his mind that was exactly how *The Lord of the Rings* grew and worked. He had not constructed a design. Instead he had tried 'to create a situation in which a common greeting would be *elen síla lúmenn' omentielmo.*' Literary critics might not believe him, but philologists (if any were left) ought to know better.

Atta, Attila: what's in a name? One answer is, a total revaluation of history. It is instructive to look at older and newer editions of Edward Gibbon's *Decline and Fall of the Roman Empire* (first published 1776–88). Gibbon knew the Goths from many Roman and Greek historians, including Jordanes, but these were his only sources of information and he could not imagine another one. 'The memory of past events,' he remarked with classically-educated superciliousness, 'cannot long be preserved, in the frequent and remote emigrations of illiterate Barbarians.' As for the great Gothic king of the fourth century, he said, 'The name of Hermanric is almost buried in oblivion.' It did not stay buried. 'Hermanric' turned up in recognisable form in *Beowulf* (not printed till 1815) as *Eormenric*. The same name and man, with little stories attached, appeared also in the Old English poems *Deor* and *Widsith*. As *Ermenrich* he survived into the Middle High German romances of *Dietrichs Flucht*, *Alpharts Tod*, and many others. Most powerfully, *Jormunrekkr* turned out to be a most prominent character in the Old Norse poems of the *Elder Edda*, which had lain unnoticed in an Icelandic farmhouse till the 1640s, and not been published in full till Rasmus Rask did the job in 1818. The 'illiterate Barbarians' were not as forgetful as Gibbon thought. They could at least remember names, and even if these had been affected by sound-changes in the same way as other words, no archaic poet produced anything as false as Gibbon's '(H)ermanric.' From the joint evidence of old poems in English, Norse and German one could in fact deduce that the king's name, though never recorded in Gothic, must have been *Aírmanareiks*.

And, as with 'Attila,' there is a thrill of old passion lurking in the name, buried though this may be in editors' footnotes and the inferences of scholarly works. The tales of Ermanaric's death vary. He committed suicide (round AD 375) for fear of the Huns, says an early Roman source. Jordanes tells a more complicated story of treachery, punishment and revenge. The Old Norse poems, more grisly and more personal, insist that Ermanaric was attacked by his brothers-in-law for murdering their sister, and was left after their death under a hail of Gothic stones—for on them no weapon would bite—to survive as a *heimnár* or 'living corpse,' a trunk with both arms and legs cut off. This last tale seems totally unlikely. But it does preserve some agreement over names and incidents with Jordanes: maybe something peculiar and tragic *did* take place during the collapse of the Gothic Empire in the fourth century. To the philologist who compared these versions there was a further charm in guessing what strange chains of transmission and quirks of national bias had transformed king into villain. Had the defeated Goths cast him as a scapegoat? Had he been made a wife-murderer to gloss over the feelings of those Goths who changed sides and joined the 'Easterlings,' calling the Hunnish king their 'little father'? Had Crimean Goths sung lays of Ermanaric to Norsemen of the Varangian Guard in the courts of the Greek emperor? Tolkien followed these inquiries closely, buying for instance the volumes of Hermann Schneider's *Germanische Heldensage* as they came out 1928–34, and claiming in 1930 that Gothic was being studied under his direction not only for sound-laws but 'as a main source of the poetic inspiration of ancient England and the North.' As he said in the letter quoted above, the legends of heroes had a fascination in themselves; they were also part of 'a rational and exacting discipline.'

Philology illuminated the Dark Ages. Certainly, when it comes to Gothic chieftains, J. B. Bury's revised edition of Gibbon (in 1896) proceeds with a new caution! But the essential point—it is a point which Tolkien's academic predecessors had signally failed to grasp, with consequent ruin for their subject—lies in the immense stretch of the philological imagination. At one extreme scholars were drawing conclusions from the very *letters* of a language: they had little hesitation in ascribing texts to Gothic or Lombardic authors, to West Saxons or Kentishmen or Northumbrians, on the evidence of sound-changes recorded in spelling. At the other extreme they were prepared to pronounce categorically on the existence or otherwise of nations and empires on the basis of poetic tradition or linguistic spread. They found information, and romance, in songs and fragments everywhere. The *Lex Burgundionum* of King Gundobad opened, as had been known for centuries, with a list of royal ancestors, Gibica, Gundomar, Gislaharius, Gundaharius. It took philology to equate nos. 1, 3 and 4 with the Gifica, Gíslhere and Gúthhere of Old English poems, nos. 1 and 4 with the Gibeche and Gunther of the Germans' epic, the *Nibelungenlied*. Simultaneously it became apparent that the epic had a kernel of truth: the Huns *had* wiped out a Burgundian king and army in the 430s (as Gibbon had vaguely noted), some of the names *were* authentic, there had been a continuing tradition of poetry from fifth to twelfth centuries, even if it had all vanished and never been written down. Sidonius Apollinaris, bishop of Clermont, indeed mentioned the Burgundians' songs with distaste in a sixth-century lyric. 'The learned and eloquent Sidonius,' Gibbon calls him. 'How gladly would we now give all his verses for ten lines of the songs in which these "long-haired seven-foot high, onion-eating barbarians" celebrated, it may be, the openhandedness of Gibica, or perhaps told how, in that last terrible battle, their fathers had fallen fighting round Gundahari,' wrote R. W. Chambers more sourly. The change of viewpoint marks an enormous if temporary shift of poetic and literary interest from Classical to native. It also shows how philology could seem, to some, the 'noblest of sciences,' the key to 'spiritual life,' certainly 'something much greater than a misfit combination of language plus literature.'

'Asterisk-Reality'

Nevertheless Sidonius's poems *had* survived, and the Burgundian epics hadn't. There was an image forming in many men's minds of the days when an enormous Germanic empire had stretched from the Baltic to the Black Sea, only to go down before the Huns and disperse into settlements everywhere from Sweden to Spain—but the image remained tantalisingly on the edge of sight. 'The ill-grace of fate has saved hardly anything . . . of the poetry possessed by the eighth, seventh and earlier centuries,' lamented Jacob Grimm and his brother Wilhelm. 'It grieves me to say it,' said Axel Olrik, 'the old *Biarkamál*, the most beloved and most honoured of songs in all the North, is not known to us in the form it had.' 'Alas for the lost lore, the annals and old poets,' wrote Tolkien, referring indeed to Virgil but by analogy to the sources of *Beowulf*. Gudbrand Vigfusson and F. York Powell, editing the *Corpus Poeticum Boreale*, the whole poetry of the North, in the 1880s, might look back on past ages and see the 'field of Northern scholarship' as 'a vast plain, filled with dry bones,' up and down which there walked 'a company of men, doing their best to set these bones in order, skull by skull, thigh by thigh, with no hope or thought of the breath that was to shake this plain with the awakening of the immortal dead.' But though philology did come and breathe life into the dry bones of old poems, filling history with the reverberations of forgotten battles and empires, still there was a point beyond which it could not go; old languages could be understood, old stories edited and annotated, but living speakers could not be found. Nor were the poems left usually the poems most ardently desired.

That is why the characteristic activity of the philologist came, in the end, to be 'reconstruction.' This might be no more than verbal. From the circumstance that English and German both change the vowel of 'man' in the plural to 'men' or *Männer*, you could infer that Primitive Germanic, of which not one word has ever been recorded, would have said **maniz*, producing as usual 'i-mutation.' The * is the sign of the reconstructed form, proposed by August Schleicher in the 1860s and used widely ever since. On a higher level you might reconstruct a language. Schleicher indeed wrote a little fable in 'Indo-European,' that 'common source' for Sanskrit, Latin and Greek which Sir William Jones had suggested. *Avis, jasmin varna na ã ast, dadarka akvams*, it began, 'A sheep, which had no wool on it, saw a horse . . .' Schleicher's colleagues were not much impressed, and indeed the researchers of Verner, Brugmann and de Saussure in the 1870s prompted H. Hirt to offer a corrected version of it some years later; no language changed as quickly in the 1870s as Primitive Indo-European, ran the philological joke. But the method itself was not seriously questioned, only the answer reached. In between these two extremes an editor might find himself rewriting a poem. *Eorl sceal on éos bæge, worod sceal getrume ridan*, says the Old English poem *Maxims I*, 'earl shall on horse's back, warband (*worod*) ride in a body.' Most warbands in Old English history marched on their feet; and anyway *worod* fails to keep up the poetic alliteration. *Éored* is the proper word here, say the editors, and it means 'a troop of cavalry,' being related to the word *eoh*, 'horse,' cp. Latin *equus*. It's true that the word is used by itself only twice elsewhere in Old English, and only once correctly—the word and idea must have become unfamiliar. But that is no deterrent. The post-philological editor can assume he knows more, indeed knows better than the native speaker or scribe, if not the original poet—another reason, be it said, for beliefs like Tolkien's, that he had a cultivated sympathy with the authors of *Beowulf* or *Sir Gawain* or *The Reeve's Tale* which even the poet's contemporaries had not and which would certainly never be reached by straight 'literary criticism.'

Examples could be multiplied almost indefinitely: it is impossible to avoid mentioning the fact that the very core and kernel of *Beowulf*-criticism in the last hundred years has been the story of 'the fall of the house of the Scyldings,' which, as it happens, neither the poet nor any other ancient writer ever got round to explaining, but which was 'reconstructed' in great and (to my mind) totally convincing detail by a succession of scholars up to R. W. Chambers. But the vital points to grasp are these:

(1) The thousands of pages of 'dry as dust' theorems about language-change, sound-shifts and *ablaut*-gradations were, in the minds of most philologists, an essential and natural basis for the far more exciting speculations about the wide plains of 'Gothia' and the hidden, secret trade-routes across the primitive forests of the North, *Myrkviðr inn ókunni*, 'the pathless Mirkwood' itself. You could not have, you would never have got the one without the other.

(2) In spite of the subject's apparent schizophrenia and the determination of its practitioners to make nothing easy, philology was, for a time, the cutting edge of all the 'soft' or 'behavioural' sciences, literature, history, sociology and anthropology at once. That is why it attracted such a following and why Jacob Grimm, for instance, could hope to sell his dictionary, the *Wörterbuch der deutschen Sprache*, to a mass-audience as something designed for entertainment.

(3) In this entire process the thing which was perhaps eroded most of all was the philologists' sense of a line between imagination and reality. The whole of their science conditioned them to the acceptance of what one might call "*-*" or 'asterisk-reality,' that which no longer existed but could with 100 per cent certainty be inferred.

(4) In a sense, the non-existence of the most desired objects of study created a romance of its own. If we had the lost Gothic 'Ermanaric-lays' we might think little of them, but find them lame, crude or brutal; quite likely, the very first version of the *Nibelungenlied* (composed in the ashes of the Burgundian kingdom) was just an attempt by the poet to cheer himself up. But the fact that these things do not exist, hover forever on the fringe of sight, makes them more tantalising and the references to them more

thrilling. There is a book by R. M. Wilson called *The Lost Literature of Medieval England*, which Tolkien must often have read. *The Lost Literature of Dark-Age Europe*, however, would be a title almost too painful for words. Still, it would cover plenty of material. The best lines about King Arthur are not the long explicit descriptions of the later medieval romances, but those in the almost deliberately uninformative Welsh triads, e.g. from the Black Book of Carmarthen:

> Bet y March, bet y Guythur,
> bet y Gugaun Cledyfrut;
> anoeth bid   bet y Arthur

> 'There is a grave for March, a grave for Gwythur,
> a grave for Gwgawn Red-sword;
> the world's wonder a grave for Arthur.'

As for Old English, my guess is that the most stirring lines to Tolkien must have come, not even from *Beowulf*, but from the fragment *Waldere*, where an unknown speaker reminds the hero that his sword was given by Theodoric to Widia 'because Wayland's child let him out of captivity, hurried him out of the hands of the monsters.' Somewhere in the Dark Ages, this seems to suggest, there must have been a legend, a story of how the Gothic king *Thiudoreiks was stolen away to the land of giants, to be rescued after long adventures by his faithful retainers Widia and Hildebrand. Why did the giants take him, where and how did they live, what were their relations with humanity? Once upon a time many people must have known the answers: the story survives in a decadent form in the medieval German romances of *Das Eckenlied*, *Sigenot*, *Laurin* and others, while there is an intensely irritating scrap of a Middle English poem on the subject tucked into a dull sermon on humility:

> Summe sende ylues, and summe sende nadderes:
> summe sende nikeres, the bi den watere wunien.
> Nister man nenne, bute Ildebrand onne.

> 'Some sent elves, and some sent serpents,
> some sent sea-monsters, that live by the water.
> No one knew any of them, but Hildebrand alone.'

What must it have been like in Old English—a poem not about monsters erupting on humanity, as in *Beowulf*, but about men going into the heart of the monsterworld, for adventures in the 'Ettenmoors' themselves! But fate had snatched that prospect (almost) into utter oblivion.

The wilderness of dragons, the shrewedness of apes

Probably the most disheartening conclusion to be drawn from this brief review of intellectual history is that the history of English studies in British and American universities has been forever marred by incomprehension and missed opportunities. Professor D. J. Palmer has shown how the birth of the Oxford English School in particular was accompanied by desperate struggles between language and literature, philologists and critics, ending not in mutual illumination but in a compromise demarcation of interests. Quite possibly the philologists were most to blame in this. Peter Ganz, Professor of German at Oxford, has pointed out that Jacob Grimm's chief intellectual defect was a refusal to generalise. Indeed as he neared the end of his *Teutonic Mythology* (four volumes in the translation of J. S. Stallybrass, and 1887 pages) Grimm wrote a Preface referring to himself as a gleaner, whose observations he left to 'him who, standing on my shoulders, shall hereafter get into full swing the harvesting of this great field.' But actually there was no field left to harvest; while few would relish the thought of spending a lifetime putting someone else's observations in order, without the fun of first collecting them! So the impetus of philology ran out in a series of Primers and Readers and Grammars, endless academic brickmaking without any sign of an architect. No wonder the early critics got annoyed. On the other hand they showed little magnanimity, or even curiosity, once they got control.

The overt result for the young Tolkien must have been that, when he returned from World War I to Oxford University in 1919, he found himself once again in a battle being fought by two sides from deep entrenchments, and one whose stalemates were as unlikely to be broken as the greater ones of Ypres or the Somme by frontal offensives. Still, both sides kept trying them. Tolkien did his best to make peace. His 1930 'manifesto' led at least to the elimination of some academic 'No Man's Land,' during the syllabus campaign of 1951 he even emerged from his trench to fraternise with the enemy (till C. S. Lewis stopped him). But a covert result may have been that he gave up hope, at least from time to time, of penetrating other people's vested interests and making them understand the appeal of the subjects he would have liked to teach. His jokes on the subject get wryer, his gestures of rapprochement—'the boundary line between linguistic and literary history is as imaginary as the equator—a certain heat is observable, perhaps, as either is approached' or 'the "pure philologist who cannot do literature" . . . is as rare as the unicorn'—these become more perfunctory and finally disappear. What was possibly a natural bent towards reserve became more pronounced; it is hard to escape the feeling that in some of the interviews given after celebrity had arrived Tolkien was still liable to give easy or unnoticedly ambiguous answers to save the trouble of explaining something which he knew had proved incomprehensible many times before. *The Hobbit* and *The Lord of the Rings* had made his point, whether it had been intellectually apprehended or not; and the hostile or even malignant reaction it evoked from so many on the 'lit.' side was only what he might have expected.

Indeed, to go back to the animus *The Lord of the Rings* created: it is striking that next to the books' sheer success the thing that irritated reviewers most was their author's obstinate insistence on talking about language as if it might be a subject of interest. 'The invention of languages is the foundation,' Tolkien had said. 'The "stories" were made rather to provide a world for the languages than the reverse.' 'Invention' of course comes from Latin *invenire*, 'to find'; its older sense, as Tolkien knew perfectly well, was 'discovery.' If one were to say of nineteenth-century philology that 'the discovery of languages was its foundation,' one would be stating literal truth; as often, probably, Tolkien was playing with words, juxtaposing the languages he had made up out of his own head with those that others had found or 'reconstructed' all over the world, so aligning himself yet again with his professional inheritance. Meanwhile the second sentence, though no doubt personally true again, might almost have been said of Ermanaric or Theodoric or the nineteenth-century vision of a 'historical' King Arthur. An element of generalisation underlay the particular application to Tolkien's own case.

This remained completely unperceived by his critics. 'He has explained that he began it to amuse himself, as a philological game,' translated Edmund Wilson. 'An overgrown fairy story, a philological curiosity—that is, then, what *The Lord of the Rings* really is.' Philology, you note, is peculiar but not serious. Lin Carter (who prepared for his commentary on Tolkien by looking up 'philology' in 'the dictionary,' to little profit—maybe it was the wrong dictionary) professed the same opinion even more blankly, if kindly, by claiming that Tolkien was really interested in 'the eternal verities of human nature,' and that the appendices of *The Lord of the Rings* needed to be seen that way and not just as 'the outgrowth of a don's scholarly hobbies.' The idea could be right, but the notion of 'scholarly hobbies' is singularly naïve. Neil D. Isaacs, also writing in Tolkien's defence, took the blunder on by asserting that 'Tolkien's own off-hand remarks about the importance of philology to the creative conception of the trilogy need not be taken too seriously,' and R. J. Reilly put the tin lid on the whole discussion by saying, in attempted refutation of Edmund Wilson, that *The Lord of the Rings* can't have been a philological game because it's too serious, and therefore, seemingly, cannot possibly be philology. 'No one ever exposed the nerves and fibres of his being in order to make up a language; it is not only insane but unnecessary.'

Like the reviewers quoted at the start of this chapter, Mr Reilly here makes a factual statement about humanity which is factually wrong. The aberration he talks about may not be common, but is not unprecedented.

August Schleicher exposed the nerves and fibres of his being to make up Primitive Indo-European, and had them shredded for his trouble. Willy Krogmann, of the University of Hamburg, not only came to the conclusion that the Old High German *Hildebrandslied* (the oldest German heroic poem) must originally have been composed in Lombardic, a West Germanic language surviving outside '*-reality' only in a handful of names, but also reconstructed the language and rewrote the poem, publishing his new edition as late as 1959. No one, as far as I know, went so far as to reconstruct the Burgundian Nibelung-story, the first Ostrogothic Ermanaric-lay, or the Danish *Ur-Beowulf*; but such thoughts were in many minds. The only extant Gothic poem is by Tolkien, 'Bagme Bloma,' in *Songs for the Philologists*. The drives towards creativity do not all emanate from the little area already mapped by 'literary' criticism. Awareness of this fact should have aroused a certain humility, or anyway caution, in Tolkienian commentators.

As it is, some of Tolkien's earliest writings seem to carry a certain foreboding truth. It has already been remarked that he tended to open learned articles with attacks on, or ripostes to, the 'literature' or the 'criticism' of his particular subject, whether this was Chaucer or the *Ancrene Wisse* or translators of *Beowulf*. Probably the sharpest and most revealing instance comes in the British Academy lecture on 'The Monsters and the Critics,' as Tolkien moves on from the melancholy state of *Beowulf* criticism as a whole to the remarks of W. P. Ker and then of R. W. Chambers— philologists whom Tolkien respected but who he thought had given too much away to the other side. 'In this conflict between plighted troth and the duty of revenge,' wrote Chambers, of a subject the *Beowulf*-poet had neglected for the sake of monsters, 'we have a situation which the old heroic poets loved, and would not have sold for a wilderness of dragons.' 'A wilderness of dragons!' exploded Tolkien, repeating the phrase and grasping instantly its deliberate syntactic ambiguity (between phrases like 'a field of cows' and phrases like 'a pride of lions'):

> There is a sting in this Shylocklan plural, the sharper for coming from a critic, who deserves the title of the poet's best friend. It is in the tradition of the Book of St. Albans, from which the poet might retort upon his critics: 'Yea, a desserte of lapwynges, a shrewednes of apes, a raffull of knaues, and a gagle of gees.'

Geese, knaves, apes, lapwings: these formed Tolkien's image of the literary critic, and they are emblematic respectively of silliness, fraud, mindless imitation and (see Horatio in *Hamlet* V ii) immaturity. But there is a multiple barb on the second phrase, the 'shrewednes of apes.' For 'shrewednes,' like most words, has changed its meaning, and as with 'literature' Tolkien thought the changes themselves significant. Nowadays it means (*OED* again) 'Sagacity or keenness of mental perception or discrimination; sagacity in practical affairs.' Once upon a time it meant 'maliciousness,' with particular reference to feminine scolding or nagging. No doubt the transit came via such phrases as 'a shrewd blow,' first a blow which was meant to hurt, then one that did hurt, then one that was accurately directed, and so on. In all these senses Tolkien's remark was 'shrewd' itself. It creates a vivid if exaggerated picture of the merits and demerits of the literary profession seen en bloc: undeniably clever, active, dexterous (so exemplifying 'shrewdness' in the modern sense), but also bitter, negative and far too fond of 'back-seat driving' (see 'shrewed' in the old sense)—overall, too, apish, derivative, cut off from the full range of human interests. It would be a pity for his claim to ring true. But the history of reactions to Tolkien has tended to uphold it. One can sum up by saying that whether the hostile criticism directed at *The Lord of the Rings* was right or wrong—an issue still to be judged—it was demonstrably compulsive, rooted only just beneath the surface in ancient dogma and dispute.

RICHARD L. PURTILL

Myth and Story

Though Tolkien's work has, as we have seen, a deep affinity with traditional myth, it is "packaged" and "marketed" as fantasy or even science fiction. Yet the market for Tolkien's work is far wider than the market for other kinds of fantasy or science fiction: evidently some readers have a taste for Tolkien that does not extend to other writers who seem superficially similar to him. We can gain a better understanding of both Tolkien and myth if we examine the nature of fantasy and science fiction, how Tolkien's work is like and unlike other work in these genres, and how fantasy and science fiction are related to myth.

Historically it might be argued that science fiction is a subdivision of the older and broader category of fantasy. But in terms of recent history, fantasy as a publishing category grew out of science fiction and still has close ties with it. Modem science fiction is usually thought of as having its origins in the 1920s when an editor named Hugo Gernsbeck began a magazine that featured stories about the future and the marvelous scientific discoveries and inventions that might shape it. Appropriately, the magazine was named *Amazing Stories*.

At first *Amazing Stories* and its imitators seemed to be only another ripple in the flood of magazine fiction printed on cheap pulp paper with garish and colorful covers—generically, pulp magazines, or "pulps." These

From *J. R. R. Tolkien: Myth, Morality, and Religion* by Richard L. Purtill. © 1984 by Richard L. Purtill.

magazines were a major source of entertainment in pre-television America, and appealed to much the same audience as television does today. There were romance "pulps," pulps for mysteries, spy stories, war stories, Westerns, and even more specialized categories, such as sea stories or "air war" stories.

But gradually science fiction pulps began to distinguish themselves from other pulp magazines. Their readers were far more intelligent and well educated than the average pulp reader and showed a tendency to form groups and clubs to discuss and promote their favorite form of reading. Gradually the quality of stories rose, and stories began to exhibit genuine scientific knowledge as well as a "sense of wonder" that went far beyond the naive awe at the wonders of science characteristic of the early science fiction magazines.

Very little real science fiction was appearing in book form at this time. H. G. Wells in England was publishing occasional novels and short stories that were genuine science fiction. The stories of Jules Verne were still popular, and a few other writers, such as Olaf Stapledon, were struggling to express their ideas in this form. But by and large, modem science fiction was a magazine phenomenon, and writers like Robert Heinlein and Isaac Asimov who are bestselling authors today learned their trade writing for the early science fiction pulps.

What is science fiction? Giving a definition of anything so complex is difficult. The trouble is that any simple definition will have too many exceptions, and any definition without exceptions will be as complex as a legal contract. The reason for the complexity is the same in both cases—the need to close up all the loopholes and take care of all the borderline cases. Rather than a formal definition, I will give a set of overlapping criteria for what makes a story science fiction. If it has many of these characteristics or has any of them to an outstanding degree, a story, whether it is written or told or filmed or performed live or on television, will be what is ordinarily called science fiction, whether those who create or present it want to call it that or not.

A story, then, is science fiction if

it is about the future; *or*
it involves space travel of a kind that has not occurred at the time the
   story is created; *or*
it involves events taking place on a planet or location other than
   Earth, but in our universe, or else in an alternative universe; *or*
it involves telepathy or other "psi" phenomena; *or*
it involves nonhuman persons or subpersonal creatures that do not
   exist in the real world but are not "supernatural" (I will call these
   "alien" persons or creatures); *or*

it involves an imaginary scientific discovery or a mechanical device of
a kind that does not exist at the time of writing and may never
exist (I will call these "fantastic" discoveries or machines).

A story that has all or most of these characteristics will be a "paradigm case,"
or standard example, of science fiction.

Stories that involve only one of the seven elements may be clearly
science fiction or on the borderline, depending on the degree to which the
element is present. Ordinary fiction may be set slightly in the future for a
variety of reasons (perhaps the author wants to describe a political situation,
a stock market manipulation, a threat of war, etc. that has never really
occurred). That does not in itself make the story science fiction. Similarly, a
story could involve space exploration techniques only slightly advanced over
present ones and use them as the basis for a spy story or a realistic novel of
industrial intrigue: the science fiction element would be too slight to make
the work science fiction. James Bond movies are often described as having
"science fiction gadgets" but are not thought of as being science fiction.
Scientific discoveries or marvelous machines can be used peripherally in a
realistic novel; for example, a psychological novel about the career pressures
of a doctor might involve a startling new medical discovery. Telepathy or
other psi phenomena may be used as minor elements in a gothic novel or a
detective story without making the story as a whole science fiction. Off-
Earth locations, time travel, and genuinely alien persons or creatures are
harder to assimilate into realistic fiction, but when such elements are
outweighed by treatment and other plot elements characteristic of
"mainstream" fiction, we hesitate to label the result science fiction.

On the other hand, even one science fiction element, if it is important
enough to the story, can make us think of the work as a whole as science
fiction. A good test is to ask what the book as a whole is "about." If it is
reasonable to say that the book is "about" space travel, time travel, telepathy,
and so on (even though it may be "about" other things too, such as courage,
sexual equality, or religion), then it seems reasonable to call the work science
fiction.

This raises two questions: what part must *science* play in science fiction,
and what part must *ideas* play in science fiction, as opposed to, say, adventure
or character. First, the part that science must play: you can insist that a
science fiction story contain scientific elements that are extrapolated from or
at least compatible with present-day scientific knowledge; if you do, you are
not defining science fiction as it is ordinarily understood but redefining it in
a narrower way.

The fact is that, if science appears at all, in much science fiction it
appears as a *means*. As we all know, science has already enabled us to travel

in space and may enable us to travel much farther and faster. The only locations for human activity that we know to exist are other planets of our own star and other stars, and our only realistic hope of reaching them is by the further development of science and technology. Time travel is quite likely not possible, but if it were, only science offers much hope of attaining it. If telepathy and other psi phenomena are fact, we count on science to discover it, and if they can be further developed, science seems to offer the best hope of doing so. Any alien persons or animals that exist are most likely to be discovered by science, and if none exist, science is most likely to create them. Marvelous discoveries or mechanisms are something science has given us in the past and is sure to give us again. The future, of course, will not be brought about by science, but in all likelihood science will have a great effect on the shape it takes. But science fiction today is interested mostly in the end results brought about by means of science, not in the means by which they are brought about. It would be possible, though very difficult, to write about the process by which science discovers truth and technology brings about changes, but the average science fiction story assumes that the process has been completed. Here we are in space or on another planet, or able to travel in time or read minds; we have encountered the aliens or made the fantastic discovery or invented the fantastic machine—now what?

What happens then may be a straight adventure story. On the other hand, it may be a story that develops the implications of the science fiction situation: what happens as a result of space or time travel, how telepathy or the marvelous machine works and how it affects society, the problems raised by the alien being or the alien planet. I will call this kind of story a *gimmick* story. Or a story may discuss the great philosophical questions that have plagued human beings since they first began to think: problems about religion, about human freedom, about human identity, and about surviving death. Problems of right and wrong for the individual and for society are often treated in science fiction, as well as problems about the scope and limits of human knowledge. A story that deals with such problems is what I call an *idea* story, but when people call science fiction "the literature of ideas" they usually mean to include what I call gimmick stories as well.

Is science fiction a literature of "ideas" in either the wide sense that includes gimmicks or in the narrow sense that includes only ideas of the kind that philosophers argue about? The only honest answer is that science fiction *can* be and often is about ideas in either the broad or the narrow sense, but it doesn't need to be. Without doing violence to the way we actually use words, you cannot deny the title science fiction to many stories not concerned with ideas in either of these senses—adventure stories, stories of character development, jokes and romps, and other "just-for-fun" stories without a trace of "idea" in either sense.

In fact, definitions of science fiction, such as "science fiction is a sub-genre of prose fiction which is distinguished from other kinds of fiction by the presence of an extrapolation of the human effects of an extrapolated science," or even "science fiction is the literature of ideas," are what logicians call *persuasive* definitions, attempts to say what the definer thinks science fiction ought to be rather than what it actually is. One could take any list of science fiction stories that have won prizes from science fiction fans or science fiction writers and find story after story that would not fit either definition. But I believe that any story on such lists would contain at least one of the several elements of science fiction we have been discussing and if it contained only one would contain it to a major degree. At any rate I am going to assume for the time being that the seven elements serve to give us a working definition of science fiction and go forward on that basis.

"Science fiction'" is often abbreviated "SF"; if it makes you feel happier to call it "speculative fiction" or "science fantasy," go right ahead and do so. My definition of a science fiction story is just a story that contains at least one of the seven elements to an important degree, and you are free to argue that what I mean by science fiction is not what you mean by real science fiction. However, I think it is pretty close to what most readers, writers, and publishers of science fiction would recognize as science fiction.

We still have one major, problem, distinguishing science fiction so defined from fantasy. Actually the fields are now and always have been so intertwined that a clear, sharp separation is almost impossible. It will help, however, to define some characteristic elements of fantasy. A story is fantasy if

> it is set in the past before recorded history begins or at some time
>   that cannot be put into a definite relationship with real time but
>   resembles past eras of history; *or*
> it involves magic (which can roughly be defined as the manipulation
>   of nature by symbolic means); *or*
> it contains persons or other creatures such that individuals like that
>   one have been the subject of myths or legends; *or*
> it involves marvelous events of which no scientific explanation is
>   given or perhaps no scientific explanation seems possible.

Take, for example, *The Lord of the Rings*. Tolkien seems to intend it to be envisioned as taking place in the long ago past of our own world, but no exact relation of his legendary "history" to real history could be given. Tolkien's world of Middle-earth contains magic, wizards, such as Gandalf, and magical objects, such as the Ring. In Middle-earth there are Elves,

Dwarves, and dragons, creatures from northern legend and myth. The marvelous events of the story are given no scientific explanation, and none seems possible for the story as told.

A story that contained only these elements, singly or in combination, would be recognized as a fantasy. If some of these elements are mixed with science fiction elements, you get mixed stories, which tend to be classified according to which elements are most prominent. For whatever reason, many of the best women writers of science fiction, Leigh Brackett, Catherine L. Moore, Andre Norton, Marion Zimmer Bradley, and Carolyn Cherryh, for instance, have tended to mix fantasy elements with science fiction elements in their writing. Usually a scientific explanation of the "magic" is offered, and although the cultures they write of are like those in our human past, they are often set in the future or on other planets, and this is usually enough to get their stories accepted as science fiction rather than fantasy.

Some symbols are extremely potent: the presence of a spaceship is almost enough by itself to make us feel that the story is science fiction; the presence of a dragon almost enough to classify a story as fantasy. Anne McCaffrey gives a science fiction background to her dragonrider stories, but many readers seem to regard them as fantasy rather than science fiction, so powerful is the dragon as a symbol. However, most of the supposed irreconcilable differences between science fiction and fantasy (science fiction deals with the possible, fantasy with the impossible; science fiction is logical, fantasy is not) can be proved by many counterexamples not to exist.

To return to science fiction, there are many ways in which it can be subdivided. We have already mentioned adventure, gimmick, and idea stories; of course these are not mutually exclusive, and some of the best science fiction contains all three elements. Often we are most aware of the idea element in a story when we disagree with it: non-Christians object to the religious ideas in C. S. Lewis's "space trilogy" (and his Narnian fantasy stories). But unless we are extremely hidebound, which most readers of science fiction are not, we can enjoy reading about ideas even if we disagree with them.

Before we leave the question of to what extent science fiction is the literature of ideas, one final comment; it will not do as a definition of science fiction, for the reasons given, but it does express an important truth about science fiction: ideas *are* important in a lot of science fiction, and if you want to write a story involving ideas, science fiction or fantasy is probably your best choice. Lots of thinking about society and its problems has taken the form of science fiction: *utopian* stories, which picture an ideal society, or *dystopian* stories, which warn of how bad society could become. But science fiction has been used to express ideas about other important topics, religion, for example. One of the most influential Christian thinkers in the twentieth century was C. S. Lewis, and some of his most influential books are a science fiction trilogy and series of fantasy stories for children. Plenty of people have written antireligious science fiction or fiction expressing doubts and problems about religion, for example, the late James Blish. Science fiction is a natural vehicle for exploring ethics and for examining alternative lifestyles, or for whatever other ideas you want to explore.

Two things ought to be noted. First, science fiction, like philosophy, challenges our assumptions and preconceptions. If you plan to write a story challenging current thinking, you are far more likely to get it published if it is science fiction. A good deal of mainstream literature simply affirms values people already have—in fact, that is probably one of the social functions of literature. But in its constant search for new ideas, science fiction is ready to look at any challenge to or reversal of accepted ideas. The second thing to be aware of is that a story cannot *prove* or even *support* any idea. It cannot cite data, for in fiction the data can be invented to suit the author. If it gives detailed arguments or chains of reasoning, it ceases to be a story and becomes a disguised philosophical treatise. What a story *can* do is help us to *understand* an idea and help us see what it feels like to hold that idea.

There are other ways of categorizing science fiction that cut across the classification into adventure, gimmick, and idea stories. Take, for instance, stories of *exploration*. The exploration may be of strange planets, of different eras of human history, of other dimensions, and so on. The focus may be on the physical characteristics of the strange environment or the alien plants and animals or the alien persons that are encountered. An exploration story may be sheer adventure—one narrow escape after another from menaces contained in the alien environment. An exploration story can also be a gimmick story, in which the chief focus is on the curious and unique elements of the environment, which may pose intellectual as well as physical challenges. Or the exploration may be used to bring out ideas: the exploration itself may even be a kind of physical analogue of the search for truth or wisdom. C. S. Lewis, in the first two volumes of his "space trilogy," uses brilliantly imagined pictures of Mars and Venus essentially as backgrounds for dramas of ideas. But the physical background and the imagined inhabitants are vivid and exciting in their own right as well as being closely tied to the ideas of the story.

A kind of story that can overlap with the exploration story is the story of *social structure*. As suggested in some of the comments on the exploration story, one of the exotic elements is often the alien social structure. Where this is a major focus in an exploration story, the story fits into both categories, exploration and social structure. But many stories of social structure are set in the familiar environment of Earth and cannot be classified as stories of exploration without unduly stretching the meaning of "exploration."

The social structure can be used merely to create adventures for the protagonist: the society may have a "guild of assassins" or a dueling code merely to pose a threat to the life of the hero or heroine. Or ingenious social arrangements can be worked out merely for their intrinsic interest, making the story a gimmick story. But very often a story of social structure is a device to make an oblique comment on our own society. It is easy for a story of that kind to degenerate into a treatise or a tract, as indeed most classical stories of utopias and dystopias do at some point or other.

Another important kind of science fiction story is the *gadget* story, which centers around some marvelous machine or quasi-mechanical device. Isaac Asimov's robot stories can be classified mainly as gadget stories, and depending on the story, Asimov may be using the robots merely to tell a story of adventure or to explore the technical problems involved in "robotics" or to comment on social and ethical or even religious issues. And of course the gadget story may be combined with the exploration or social structure story.

Finally, some science fiction stories can only be described, as *psychological* stories, or stories of character. Science fiction is often criticized for neglecting characterization, and the story of character change and development seems much more at home in contemporary, realistic fiction. But there have always been some science fiction stories that concentrate on psychology or character development. Stories of "supermen," such as Stapledon's *Odd John*, are often basically psychological studies of the alienated or unusual human individual. (Incidentally, I would classify "superman" stories as involving the "alien" theme, since supermen are by definition more than and other than human.)

Now how does all this relate to mythology? Plainly, if it is simply regarded as a kind of story, myth has a great deal in common with science fiction, and especially with fantasy. Myth, like fantasy, tends to be backward-looking, to set its stories in the remote past. Instead of space travel, it tends to have magical or mysterious means of travel, such as those employed by the gods in Homer or the mysterious gates to the Other World or Faërie or the Underworld found in some legends and fairy tales. Instead of a distant planet, a myth may be set in heaven or hell, Olympus or Hades, the land of Faërie or the Western Isles.

Time travel as such does not come into myth, though there are "Rip van Winkle" stories in which a mortal wanders into an enchanted realm and returns to the world to find that many years have passed in what seemed a short time in the other world. In many myths and legends, gods or elves seem to have powers like those that would be called "psi" powers nowadays. Gods, elves, dragons, gryphons, and so on fit the classification of "alien" persons, whereas such things as magical rings and swords and helms and cloaks replace the machines of science fiction.

Myths served many functions in more primitive societies, and at least some of them were very similar to some of the purposes served today by science fiction and fantasy. Sheer entertainment is one such purpose. People have always enjoyed stories about fantastic and far-off things and people, whether in the form of travelers' tales, medieval and Renaissance romances, or today's science fiction and fantasy films, like *Star Wars* or *Dragonslayer.* One element in Homer's *Odyssey*, for example, is simply a story of adventure and exploration.

The element I have called the gimmick element is not especially strong in the higher mythologies, where gods or magical objects seem to achieve their effects simply by being what they are. But in fairy tales there is often a sort of gimmick element in that the protagonist of the tale has a problem to solve in the face of what seems like overwhelming odds. How is the youngest son to win fame and fortune and the hand of the princess? How is the princess to recover her beloved who has been magicked away to some enchanted realm? Often the solution is a mixture of nature, wit, and magical help: for example, the princess takes a job as a scullery maid in the enchanted palace where her beloved is held but then is befriended by an enchanted creature she has been kind to.

Obviously myths have been used to convey ideas of all kinds. Stories about the marital wranglings of Zeus and Hera or Aphrodite and Hephaestus could be used to make a comment on human husbands and wives. The protagonists of the stories about demigods and heroes often express cultural values. The heroes of Greek myth are often quick-witted as well as strong and brave. Odysseus is the paradigm of the thinker as hero, but even Hercules is more than a strongman. He cleanses the Augean stables by directing a river to do his work, for example, which needs ingenuity as well as strength.

Tolkien's mythology as expressed in *The Silmarillion* and in the background myths of *The Hobbit* and *The Lord of the Rings* probably owes most to his study of genuine original myth. Many writers on Tolkien have mentioned his debt to the myths and legends of northern Europe, but an influence equally strong or even stronger is Greek and Roman mythology. As we will see, Tolkien's Valar have a greater resemblance to the Olympian gods than to the Scandinavian gods such as Odin and Thor. For the details of his stories Tolkien has borrowed from many myths, but Greek and Roman language and literature kept a strong hold on his imagination. He writes in a letter that "I was brought up in the Classics and first discovered the sensation of literary pleasure in Homer." Elsewhere he comments on the way in which the "marvelous aesthetic" of the Greek language ties together the Greek mythology into a unity: this was a major objective of his own, making his invented languages give a unity to his mythic system. Later on, at the period when he wrote *The Lord of the Rings* and afterwards, Tolkien read at least some science fiction and modern fantasy. In 1967 he wrote:

> I read quite a lot—or more truly, try to read many books (notably so-called Science Fiction and Fantasy). But I seldom find any modern books that hold my attention. There are exceptions. I have read all that E. R. Eddison wrote, in spite of his peculiarly bad nomenclature and personal philosophy. I was greatly taken by the book that was (I believe) the runner-up when *The L.R.* was given the Fantasy Award: *Death of Grass*. I enjoy the fiction of Isaac Azimov [*sic*]. Above these I was recently deeply engaged in the books of Marie Renault, especially the two about Theseus, *The King Must Die* and *The Bull from the Sea*. A few days ago I actually received a card of appreciation from her; perhaps the piece of "fan-mail" that gives me most pleasure.

These comments, of course, were made after the writing of *The Lord of the Rings*, but they show the general *kind* of reading Tolkien enjoyed: Isaac Asimov's stories are typical science fiction (set in the future with space travel, off-Earth locations, etc.). Marie Renault's stories are based on Greek mythology, though they play down the magical and fantastic elements. Eddison's stories are set in a fantastic "alternative universe" and have a strong supernatural element.

One story we know Tolkien enjoyed before writing *The Lord of the Rings* was C. S. Lewis's Martian novel *Out of the Silent Planet*. Tolkien wrote a letter to a publisher in an effort to help Lewis get the book published.

> I read the story in the original MS, and was so enthralled that I could do nothing else until I had finished it. . . . All the part about language and poetry—the glimpses of its Malacandrian nature and form—is very well done and extremely interesting, far superior to what one usually gets from travellers in untravelled regions. The language difficulty is usually slid over or fudged. Here it not only has verisimilitude, but underlying thought . . . I should have said that the story had for the more intelligent reader a great number of philosophical and mythical implications that enormously enhanced without detracting

from the surface "adventure." I found the blend of *vera historia*
with *mythos* irresistible. There are of course certain satirical
elements, inevitable in any such traveller's tale and also a spice
of satire on similar works of "scientific" fiction.

This letter forms an interesting commentary on what Tolkien himself
tried to accomplish and did accomplish in *The Lord of the Rings*:
"philosophical and mythical implications that enormously enhanced without
detracting from the surface "adventure" . . . [a] blend of *vera historia* with
mythos" are descriptions of Tolkien's best work as well as Lewis's.

In fact Tolkien's work and Lewis's are almost unique in the successful
blending of these elements. There is plenty of science fiction that has
philosophical elements, plenty of fantasy with mythical elements, but the
blend of all three is rare. Ursula LeGuin in her Earthsea trilogy and Samuel
K. Delany in his Neveryon books approach this blend most closely.

Tolkien is on record as disliking Lewis's Narnia books and also criticizing
the concluding book of Lewis's "space trilogy," *That Hideous Strength*, partly
because of the influence Tolkien felt Charles Williams had on it.

The "space travel" trilogy . . . was basically foreign to Williams'
kind of imagination. It was planned years before when we
decided to divide: Lewis was to do space travel and I was to do
time travel. . . . Publication dates are not a good guide.
Williams' influence actually only appeared with his death: *That
Hideous Strength*, the end of the trilogy which (good though it
is in itself) I think spoiled it.

There may have been a certain element of jealousy in Tolkien's attitude
to Charles Williams. He wrote about Williams's relationship to Lewis in a
letter to his son in 1963: "We were separated first by the sudden apparition
of Charles Williams, then by his marriage." Tolkien was temperamentally, I
think, the sort of man who chooses a few close friends and sticks to them for
life, whereas Lewis was inclined to expand his circle of friends. Tolkien says
in a letter, "C. S. L. was my closest friend from about 1927 to 1940 and
remains very dear to me—his death was a grievous blow. But in fact we saw
less and less of one another after he came under the influence of Charles
Williams and still less after his very strange marriage." I am not sure that
Lewis would ever have thought of Tolkien as "my closest friend": the note of
exclusiveness is not like Lewis, but very like Tolkien.

As it happened it was the science fiction community that in an indirect
and complicated way caused much of the wide public attention that came to
The Lord of the Rings. The story was published in three books in hardcover by

Unwin in England and Houghton Mifflin in the United States. It attracted some attention but seemed to have no wide public appeal. Donald A. Wollheim, a longtime science fiction fan, writer, and editor, was at this time (1965) editor in chief of Ace Books, a firm that published inexpensive paperbacks that were in many ways the successors of the pulp magazines (Ace had started as a magazine publisher). Wollheim admired *The Lord of the Rings* and thought that it would appeal to the readers of Ace science fiction, which included some fantasy and borderline science fiction–fantasy.

What happened next is still somewhat controversial. It is described from the point of view of Tolkien and his publishers in Humphrey Carpenter's biography of Tolkien:

> . . . what Tolkien and others regarded as an American 'pirate' edition of *The Lord of the Rings* had been issued.
>
> The publishers were Ace Books, who (when challenged) alleged there was nothing illegal in their paperback, even though it was printed entirely without the permission of Tolkien or his authorised publishers, and even though no royalty payment had been offered to the author.
>
> Ace were already known as publishers of science fiction, and clearly a lot of people were going to buy their edition until an authorised paperback could be issued. An urgent request was sent to Tolkien to complete the revisions. . . .
>
> In October 1965, the "authorised" paperback of *The Lord of the Rings* was published in America. . . . Each copy carried a message from Tolkien: "This paperback edition and no other has been published with my consent and cooperation. Those who approve of courtesy (at least) to living authors will purchase it and no other."
>
> But this did not immediately produce the desired result. The Ballantine edition cost twenty cents per volume more than the Ace edition, and the American student buyers did not at first show a preference for it. Clearly something more would have to be done. . . . Tolkien himself played a prominent and efficient part in the campaign that now began . . . he began to include a note in all his replies to American readers informing them that the Ace edition was unauthorized and asking them to tell their friends. This soon had a remarkable effect. American readers not only began to refuse to buy the Ace edition but demanded . . . that booksellers remove it from their shelves.

Another point of view is given in the lively and controversial "unauthorized" biography of Tolkien by Daniel Grotta:

> One serious tactical mistake that Allen & Unwin made was in greatly underestimating the audience for *The Lord of the Rings*. The trilogy became an underground classic among science fiction and fantasy readers, many of whom could not afford $15 or more for a three-volume hardbound set. There had been a sizable paperback market for the work almost immediately after its initial publication in the mid-50s, but no paperback edition was forthcoming. This oversight by both Allen & Unwin and Houghton Mifflin created a vacuum that was filled by a less conservative publishing house, Ace Books. . . .
>
> Ace Books was and still is a major paperback publisher of popular science fiction. . . . Wollheim knew about the underground popularity of *The Lord of the Rings* and wanted to get the rights to publish it in paperback. He quickly found out that the trilogy was not copyrighted in the United States and therefore, according to him, began lengthy and frustrating negotiations with Professor Tolkien through Allen & Unwin. Allen & Unwin was unenthusiastic, and Tolkien did not respond at all. When Wollheim finally advised his publisher, A.A. Wyn, of the situation, Wyn told him to go ahead and publish the trilogy. The Ace Books edition . . . went on sale in May, 1965. . . .
>
> Ace's decision to publish the work in paperback was probably the best thing that ever happened to Tolkien. According to Donald Wollheim's wife, it "took off like a rocket," revealing the unrealized readership potential for an affordable edition of *The Lord of the Rings*. Despite the official acrimony and the charge of moral piracy, Tolkien profited handsomely from the entire affair. Technically, Ace Books was not obliged to give Tolkien a single penny for the rights to his books, but A.A. Wyn decided to set aside all the money that would have ordinarily gone to the author and establish a Tolkien Prize, which would encourage young writers of science fiction and fantasy. When Wollheim wrote to Tolkien of their intention to apply the $11,000 to a literary prize in his name, Tolkien responded and asked for the money himself. Since the agreement was between Ace and Tolkien, the entire $11,000

went directly to the professor. Ordinarily the author and
original publisher share equally in any foreign rights; with
three publishers—Allen & Unwin, Houghton Mifflin, and
Ballantine Books—this meant that Tolkien received only 25
percent of the royalties from the official American edition.
Since no other publishers were involved with Ace, Tolkien
received 100 percent.

The points not in dispute are that Tolkien's publishers had lost American
copyright protection for *The Lord of the Rings* by importing too many
"sheets" (unbound copies) of the book from England to be bound and
published in the United States, and that Ace Books was within its legal rights
in publishing a paperback edition without payment to Tolkien or his
publishers. The question in dispute is whether they were morally justified in
doing so.

Wollheim's side of the controversy, as stated in Grotta's book and
confirmed in a letter to me, is that he and others had requested paperback
rights from Tolkien's publisher and been turned down. When it came to light
that U.S. copyright protection for the work had been lost, it seemed to
Wollheim that this explained the refusal: they could not sell rights they did
not have. There seemed no reason to suppose that there would ever be an
American paperback edition authorized by Houghton Mifflin. So Wollheim
felt justified in going ahead with an Ace Books paperback edition. He was
under no legal obligation to offer any royalties to Tolkien or Houghton
Mifflin. The publisher could not have accepted any such royalties without in
effect authorizing his edition, nor could Tolkien have accepted them without
undercutting his publisher's position.

Tolkien and his publishers responded by waging a publicity campaign
which emphasized the fact that Tolkien received no royalties from the Ace
edition and by preparing a revised edition that could be protected under U.S.
copyright law. The controversy over the Ace and Ballantine editions gave
The Lord of the Rings a good deal of publicity and undoubtedly helped its
growing sales. Ace Books eventually ceased publication of its edition. In a
letter to W. H. Auden, Tolkien says:

> May I intrude into this letter a note on Ace Books, since I have
> engaged to inform "my correspondents" of the situation. They
> in the event sent me a courteous letter and I signed an
> "amicable agreement" with them to accept their voluntary
> offer under no legal obligation: to pay a royalty at 4 per cent on
> all copies of their edition sold, and not to reprint it when
> exhausted (without my consent).

In the end the whole affair has a somewhat comic aspect. Tolkien undoubtedly benefited. A paperback edition of *The Lord of the Rings* got printed in the United States that might have been published later or not at all if left to his American publishers. The controversy gave the book priceless publicity. And because the Ace payment was made directly to Tolkien, he got more of it than he would have otherwise. Standard contracts of that period gave the hardcover publisher 50 percent or so of payments for paperback publication, and 4 percent was a fairly standard royalty rate for most mass market paperbacks. Thus Tolkien got 4 percent instead of 2 percent of the money earned by the Ace paperback and, I hope, got a somewhat better deal on the Ballantine paperback than he might otherwise have.

Humphrey Carpenter, Tolkien's biographer, concluded that the whole business had done more good than harm: "Ace had unwittingly done a service to Tolkien, for they had helped lift his book from the 'respectable' hard cover status in which it had languished for some years and had put it at the top of the popular bestsellers."

To sum up our account of science fiction, fantasy, and myth in relation to Tolkien: all three have important elements in common, but each differs from the other in essential ways. Tolkien's work, though certainly not science fiction, is admired by many readers of science fiction. *The Lord of the Rings* not only is fantasy but is probably responsible for the current popularity of fantasy, which threatens to take over some of the market for science fiction. (Adult fantasy as a publishing category really started with the effort by Ballantine and other publishers to find "something like Tolkien" to satisfy the enormous market created by *The Lord of the Rings*.)

The effect of Tolkien's work on his readers has often been to restore the mythic dimension to their consciousness, even to the extent that some Tolkien enthusiasts dress in costumes and re-enact incidents from *The Lord of the Rings*. The old connection of myth and ritual has been partly restored. Tolkien may not have quite succeeded in making a mythology for *all* of England, but he has created a new mythology that lives in and for some of his readers.

Chronology

1892   John Ronald Reuel Tolkien, called Ronald, is born on January 3, the first son of Mabel Suffield Tolkien and Arthur Tolkien.

1894   Ronald's brother, Hilary Arthur Reuel, is born.

1895   Mabel and her sons return to England, partly for reason of Ronald's health; live with Suffields in Birmingham.

1896   Arthur Tolkien (father) dies of rheumatic fever in Africa.

1900   Mabel and her sons become Catholic. Ronald enters King Edward's School.

1904   Mabel Suffield Tolkien (mother) dies in November. Father Francis Morgan is designated the boys' guardian.

1910   Awarded a scholarship to study Classics at Exeter College, Oxford.

1913   Transfers from Classics to English, with emphasis in philology, and formally studies Old Norse.

1914   Gets engaged to Edith Bratt.

1915   Takes a First Class degree in English from Oxford. Enters the army.

1916   Marries Edith Bratt. Participates in the Battle of the Somme. Is invalided out of the army in November.

1917   Begins to write tales later known as *The Book of Lost Tales*. First son, John, is born.

1918   Joins the staff at the Oxford English Dictionary.

1920   Appointed Reader in English Language at Leeds University. Begins poems known as *Lays of Beleriand.* Second son, Michael, is born.

1924   Appointed Professor of English Language at Leeds. Third son, Christopher, is born.

1925   Publishes an edition of *Sir Gawain and the Green Knight* with E.V. Gordon. Is named Rawlinson and Bosworth Professor of Anglo-Saxon at Oxford University.

1929   Daughter, Priscilla, is born.

1930   Completes full draft of *The Silmarillion* (printed in *The Shaping of Middle-Earth,* 1986).

1932   C.S. Lewis reads a manuscript of *The Hobbit.* Tolkien at work on an expanded *Silmarillion* and continues to publish poems and articles.

1936   Delivers lecture, "Beowulf: The Monsters and the Critics," before British Academy. *The Hobbit* is accepted for publication.

1937   *The Hobbit* is published.

1938   *The Hobbit* is published in the U.S. and receives *New York Herald Tribune* award as best children's book of the season.

1939   Delivers lecture "On Fairy-Stories" at St. Andrews University.

1945   Named Merton Professor of English Language and Literature at Oxford University.

1948   *The Lord of the Rings* is completed.

1949   *Farmer Giles of Ham* is published.

1954   The first two volumes of *The Lord of the Rings* (*The Fellowship of the Ring* and *The Two Towers*) is published.

1955   The last volume, *The Return of the King,* is published.

1959   Retires from Oxford University.

1962   Publishes *The Adventures of Tom Bombadil,* a collection of poems.

1964   *Tree and Leaf* is published.

1965   Tolkien Society of America is founded.

1967   *Smith of Wootton Major* is published.

1971   Edith Tolkien dies, aged eighty-two.

1972   Receives honorary doctorate from Oxford University and is honored by the Queen.

1973   Dies on September 2 at age eighty-one.

Contributors

HAROLD BLOOM is Sterling Professor of the Humanities at Yale University and Henry W. and Albert A. Berg Professor of English at the New York University Graduate School. He is the author of over 20 books, including *The Anxiety of Influence* (1973), which sets forth Professor Bloom's provocative theory of the literary relationships between the great writers and their predecessors. His most recent book, *Shakespeare: The Invention of the Human* (1998), was a finalist for the 1998 National Book Award. Professor Bloom is a 1985 MacArthur Foundation Award recipient, served as the Charles Eliot Norton Professor of Poetry at Harvard University in 1987–88, and has received honorary degrees from the universities of Rome and Bologna. In 1999, Professor Bloom received the prestigious American Academy of Arts and Letters Gold Medal for Criticism.

THOMAS J. GASQUE is an English scholar and critic who has published several articles on fantasy fiction including an original essay on J. R. R. Tolkien for the collection *Tolkien and the Critics: Essays on J. R. R. Tolkien's The Lord of the Rings*.

PAUL H. KOCHER is an Emeritus Professor of English and Humanities at Stanford University. He has written extensively on many subjects including Christopher Marlowe, J. R. R. Tolkien, and a book on Renaissance science and religion.

ROGER SALE is a Professor of English at the University of Washington, Seattle. He is the editor of *Discussions of the Novel* and the author of *Reading Spenser* and *On Writing*.

DANIEL GROTTA-KURSKA is a literary scholar whose publications include *The Green Travel Sourcebook* and a biography of Tolkien entitled *J. R. R. Tolkien: Architect of Middle Earth*.

TIMOTHY R. O'NEILL has written many articles and technical monographs for professional journals. He is a career Army officer and a Professor of Behavioral Sciences and Leadership at the United States Military Academy.

ANNE C. PETTY has been the project editor of the Center for Educational Technology, Florida State University. Her publications include a book on Tolkien, *One Ring To Bind Them All: Tolkien's Mythology*.

NEIL D. ISAACS is a Professor in the English department at the University of Maryland. He has been the coeditor of two collections of essays on Tolkien, including *Tolkien and the Critics: Essays on J. R. R. Tolkien's* Lord of the Rings.

T. A. SHIPPEY was a student of J. R. R. Tolkien at Oxford University. He went on to become the Chair of English Language and Medieval Literature at Leeds University, which Tolkien also held early in his career. His publications include *The Road To Middle-Earth*.

RICHARD L. PURTILL is a Professor of Philosophy at Western Washington University in Bellingham. He is the author of several scholarly works, including *C.S. Lewis's Case for the Christian Faith*, *Lord of the Elves*, and *Eldild: Fantasy and Philosophy in C.S. Lewis and J. R. R. Tolkien* as well as many novels.

Bibliography

Auden, W. H. "Good and Evil in *The Lord of the Rings.*" *Tolkien Journal* 3 (1967): 5–8. Reprinted in *Critical Quarterly* 10 (1968): 138–42.

Beatie, Bruce A. "*The Lord of the Rings*: Myth, Reality, and Relevance." *Western Review* 4 (Winter 1967): 58–59.

Becker, Alida, ed. *The Tolkien Scrapbook.* New York: Grosset and Dunlap, 1974.

Bettelheim, Bruno. *The Uses of Enchantment: The Meaning and Importance of Fairy Tales.* New York: Alfred A. Knopf, 1976.

Blissett, William. "Despots of the Rings." *South Atlantic Quarterly* 58 (Summer 1959): 448–56.

Campbell, Joseph. *The Hero with a Thousand Faces.* New York: Pantheon, 1949.

Carpenter, Humphrey. *Tolkien: A Biography.* Boston: Houghton Mifflin, 1977.

Crabbe, Katharyn F. *J. R. R. Tolkien.* New York: Frederick Ungar, 1981.

Evans, Robley. *J. R. R. Tolkien.* New York: Warner, 1972.

Giddings, Robert, ed. *J. R. R. Tolkien: This Far Land.* London: Vision, 1983.

Green, William H. "The Four-Part Structure of Bilbo's Education." *Children's Literature* 8 (1979): 133–40.

Grotta-Kurska, Daniel. *J. R. R. Tolkien: Architect of Middle Earth.* Philadelphia: Running Press, 1976.

Hall, Robert A., Jr. "Tolkien's Hobbit Tetralogy as 'Anti-Nibelungen.'" *Western Humanities Review* 32 (1978): 351–60.

Hammond, Wayne G., and Scull, Christina. *J. R. R. Tolkien, Artist & Illustrator.* Boston: Houghton Mifflin, 1995.

Hayes, Noreen and Renshaw, Robert. "Of Hobbits: *The Lord of the Rings.*" *Critique* 9 (1967): 58–66.

Helms, Randel. *Tolkien's World.* Boston: Houghton Mifflin, 1974.

Hieatt, Constance. "The Text of *The Hobbit.*" *English Studies in Canada* 7 (Summer 1981): 212–24.

Hillegas, Mark R., ed. *Shadows of Imagination: The Fantasies of C. S. Lewis, J. R. R. Tolkien, and Charles Williams.* Carbondale and Edwardsville, Illinois: Southern Illinois University Press, 1979.

Irwin, W. R. "There and Back Again: The Romances of Williams, Lewis, and Tolkien." *Sewanee Review* 69 (1961): 566–78.

Isaacs, Neil D., and Zimbardo, Rose A., eds. *Tolkien and the Critics.* Notre Dame, Indiana: University of Notre Dame Press, 1968.

Kocher, Paul H. *Master of Middle-earth: The Fiction of J. R. R. Tolkien.* New York: Houghton Mifflin, 1972.

Lobdell, Jared C., ed. *A Tolkien Compass.* La Salle, Ill.: Open Court, 1975.

Lucas, Mary R. "Review of *The Hobbit.*" *Library Journal* 63 (1938): 385.

Manlove, C. N. *Modern Fantasy: Five Studies.* Cambridge, England: Cambridge University Press, 1975.

Mathews, Richard. *Lightening from a Clear Sky: Tolkien, the Trilogy, and The Silmarillion.* San Bernardino, Calif.: Borgo, 1978.

Matthews, Dorothy. "The Psychological Journey of Bilbo Baggins." In *A Tolkien Compass,* ed. Jared C. Lobdell. LaSalle, Ill.: Open Court, 1976.

Nicol, Charles. "Reinvented Word." *Harper's,* November 1977, p. 95.

Nitzsche, Jane Chance. *Tolkien's Art: A* "Mythology for England." New York: St. Martin's Press, 1979.

Norman, Philip. "The Prevalence of Hobbits." *New York Times Magazine,* 15 January (1967): 3

Petty, Anne C. *One Ring to Bind Them All: Tolkien's Mythology.* Tuscaloosa, Alabama: University of Alabama Press, 1979.

Purtill, Richard. *Lord of the Elves and Eldild: Fantasy and Philosophy in C.S. Lewis and J. R. R. Tolkien.* Grand Rapids, Mich.: Zondervan, 1974.

Sale, Roger. "England's Parnassus: C. S. Lewis, Charles Williams, and J. R. R. Tolkien." *Hudson Review* 17 (1964): 203–25.

———. *Modern Heroism: Essays on D.H. Lawrence, William Empson and J.R.R. Tolkien.* Berkeley: University of California Press, 1973.

Salu, Mary, and Farrell, Robert T., eds. *J. R. R. Tolkien, Scholar and Storyteller: Essays in Memoriam.* Ithaca: Cornell University Press, 1979.

Shippey, T. A. *The Road to Middle-Earth.* London: George Allen and Unwin, 1982.

Spacks, Patricia Meyer. "Ethical Pattern in *Lord of the Rings.*" *Critique* 3 (1959): 30–42.

Thomson, George H. "*The Lord of the Rings*: The Novel as Traditional Romance." *Wisconsin Studies in Contemporary Literature* 8 (1967): 43–59.

West, Richard C. *Tolkien Criticism: An Annotated Checklist.* Kent, Ohio: Kent State University Press, 1970.

Wilson, Edmund. "Oo, Those Awful Orcs!" *Nation* 182 (1956): 312–13.

Yates, Jessica. "The Source of 'The Lay of Aotrou and Itroun.'" *Leaves From the Tree: J. R. R. Tolkien's Shorter Fiction.* London: The Tolkien Society, 1991.

Acknowledgments

"Tolkien: The Monsters and the Critters" by Thomas J. Gasque from *Tolkien and the Critics: Essays on J. R. R. Tolkien's* The Lord of the Rings, edited by Neil D. Isaacs and Rose A. Zimbardo. © 1968 by University of Notre Dame Press.

"Cosmic Order" by Paul H. Kocher from *Master of Middle-earth: The Fiction of J. R. R. Tolkien* by Paul H. Kocher. © 1972 by Paul H. Kocher.

"Tolkien and Frodo Baggins" by Roger Sale from *Modern Heroism: Essays on D.H. Lawrence, William Empson, & J. R. R. Tolkien* by Roger Sale. © 1973 by The Regents of the University of California.

"The Author" by Daniel Grotta-Kurska from *J. R. R. Tolkien: Architect of Middle Earth*, A Biography by Daniel Grotta-Kurska, edited by Frank Wilson. © 1976 by Running Press.

"The Individuated Hobbit" by Timothy R. O'Neill from *The Individuated Hobbit: Jung, Tolkien and the Archetypes of Middle-earth* by Timothy R. O'Neill. © 1979 by Timothy R. O'Neill.

"Tolkien's Prelude" by Anne C. Petty from *One Ring To Bind Them All: Tolkien's Mythology* by Anne C. Petty. © 1979 by The University of Alabama Press.

"A Mythology for England" by Paul H. Kocher from *A Reader's Guide To The Silmarillion* by Paul H. Kocher. © 1980 by Paul H. Kocher.

"On the Need for Writing Tolkien Criticism" by Neil D. Isaacs from *Tolkien: New Critical Perspectives*, edited by Neil D. Isaacs & Rose A. Zimbardo. © 1981 by The University Press of Kentucky.

"'Lit. and Lang.'" by T. A. Shippey from *The Road to Middle-Earth* by T. A. Shippey. © 1982 by T. A. Shippey.

"Myth and Story" by Richard L. Purtill from *J. R. R. Tolkien: Myth, Morality, and Religion* by Richard L. Purtill. © 1984 by Richard L. Purtill.

Index